EDDIE IDUOZE

LEAD
LIKE THIS!

Essential lessons from the life of Jesus
to help you transform your Church,
Company, and Community

First published 2024
© 2024 by Eddie Iduoze
British Library Cataloguing in Publication Data
A CIP catalogue record for this book is available
from the British Library.

ISBN:9-781739-098988

Cover design and page layout by David Springer

Editorial and publishing services by
The Heritage Publishers Ltd

ACKNOWLEDGEMENTS

My first debt goes to God for calling me to spiritual leadership. His grace has been sufficient.

I would like to thank all the members of Gateway Chapel for allowing me to lead them and make my mistakes in leadership without condemnation.

Toyin Onabowu, my Editor, for your patience and hard work in ensuring this book reads well. All I did was drop a piece of wood on your table, and you managed to sculpt this work of art.

To Asher Iduoze and Bethel Iduoze, my heart living outside my body. Everyone gets to go home and take a break from their Coach, but you live with yours. I am so proud of how you have emerged as young leaders.

To Bola Iduoze, the light of my life, my best friend, and my greatest supporter.

CONTENTS

CONTENTS

CONTENTS

‘From Him the whole
body [the church, in all its various
parts], joined and knitted firmly together
by what every joint supplies, when each part
is working properly, causes the body to
grow and mature, building itself
up in [unselfish] love.’

———————————

Ephesians 4:16 AMP

Jesus Christ is the most powerful and influential leader of all time. Despite what people believe about him, the message he tasked his disciples to preach to the world is still impacting billions more than 2,000 years later. Jesus demonstrated perfect leadership attributes and skills, qualities that are important for any leader's lasting success. No one can define his exceptional leadership style with words, but we can learn countless lessons from his life and ministry, and these are the focus of this book.

In today's world, many leaders expect their subordinates to perform tasks they themselves are incapable of doing, which destroys their credibility and costs them their followers' respect. Jesus led by example: whatever he expected of his disciples, he did first, both in word and practice.

Much of what is said and written about Christian leadership is not actually about leadership but about theological, expositional, hermeneutical, worship facilitation and communication skills. In addition, leadership in Christian circles today frequently gets confused with the modern celebrity concept. Where consideration is given to vital people skills and expertise, the Christian world bypasses Jesus Christ, the one role model who should be in focus, to call on secular, worldly models. When Satan wants to attack the church, he usually goes after the leadership. If he can bring down or, at least, get people to slander a prominent leader, he can discredit the entire gospel.

From the above observations, a few questions must arise:

- How do I recognize a great leader and good leadership?

- What are the pitfalls to avoid?

- Is one leadership style better than others?

- In which areas do I need to grow to be a great leader?

- How can I lead as Christ did?

These questions and more will be adequately addressed in this book as we examine Jesus' leadership styles and qualities, using them as an objective standard and framework to reflect on our leadership (beginner or experienced) and identify areas to develop into further Christlikeness. Such a framework also helps the Church discern whether a person is truly called, anointed, and raised by God to lead His people.

Was Jesus Christ a great leader?

Religion and spiritual beliefs aside, no one in history has been more discussed, worshipped, or inspired more songs, books, and artwork. Jesus created one of the world's most sustained organizations (the Church), so he is certainly a leader from whom lessons can be learned and applied in today's world.

Great leaders lead from the inside out. Jesus focused on personal leadership first in matters of character, at the core of which is integrity. Without this trait, most honest people will not follow you for long, and more importantly, you are not leading like Christ.

> *Without integrity, most honest people will not follow you for long, and more importantly, you are not leading like Christ.*

Leadership is an inside job. Skills only take you as far as your character allows, and Jesus had a pure heart and unfailing character. The harder you work on your heart and character; the more others seek to emulate you.

Great leaders are great servants. Jesus washed his disciples' feet right before his greatest challenge. Knowing his time with them was limited, he seized the opportunity to show and teach them that the greatest way to lead was by serving them. Great leaders today see themselves as serving – equipping, encouraging, and coaching – their teams to realize their potential. Leadership is about others, not you.

Great leaders balance conviction with compassion. Jesus held strong convictions and values yet showed tremendous compassion to those who did not share his convictions. Great leaders are both clear about their values and expectations and yet sensitive to the person, which engages hearts and minds and motivates followers to give their discretionary effort.

Great leaders are great storytellers. Jesus' stories have withstood the test of time, with his preferred storytelling style being the parable. Stories are richer, more powerful and longer lasting than directives or instructions. Look at your own life for relevant stories (we all have them) and turn them into coaching tools to build your team and leadership legacy.

You don't have to be great to get started, but you have to get started to be great.
Christian leadership begins with God's calling, which comes in two parts. First, God gives the desire to serve him, and second, the church recognizes the traits and gifts that qualify you for leadership, the most prominent of which is Christ-like character. To lead Christ's people, we must have walked with Christ.

May God help us be such men.

CHAPTER ONE

CHRISTIAN LEADERSHIP

Christian leadership is not rooted in worldly notions of success, such as the love of money or power, which Jesus spoke against when he emphasised the importance of serving others.

> 'But Jesus called them to Himself and said,
> 'You know that the rulers of the Gentiles lord
> it over them, and those who are great exercise
> authority over them. Yet it shall not be so
> among you; but whoever desires to become
> great among you, let him be your servant. And
> whoever desires to be first among you, let him
> be your slave — just as the Son of Man did not
> come to be served, but to serve, and to give His
> life a ransom for many.' Matthew 20:25-28

THE GOOD VERSUS THE GREAT LEADER

Leadership is the act of serving, influencing and empowering others to accomplish God's purposes. A good leader considers the interests of others when achieving their objective. A great leader is committed to raising good leaders.

Leaders are not to oppress and overpower with their authority but to serve. Jesus demonstrated this when he

> '...made Himself of no reputation, taking the
> form of a bondservant, and coming in the
> likeness of men. And being found in appearance
> as a man, He humbled Himself and became
> obedient to the point of death, even the death
> of the cross' (Philippians 2:7-8).

CHARACTERISTICS OF THE CHRISTIAN LEADER – THE BASELINE

1. LOVE

Love is central to Christianity, and every Christian leader should be driven by God's love as a minimum standard. Leaders are typically admired for great accomplishments, so the word 'love' doesn't necessarily spring to mind as a requirement. However, the power and influence of God's love cannot be overemphasized. John 3:16 clearly refers to it as the motivation behind God's reconciliation plan for the world. Jesus commanded us to love God and people (Mark 12:30-31), going further to expressly state that his disciples' identity and followership were rooted and only recognisable by their love for one another (John 13:35).

In 1 Corinthians 13, Paul talks about love's transformational nature and how it is greater than spiritual gifts like faith and hope. In other words, as the fulcrum of leadership, love changes and brings out the best in the leader and the led.

Jesus loved people: Luke 19:10

> '...for the Son of Man has come to seek and to save that which was lost.'

Jesus loved people of all ethnic and economic backgrounds. He also took great joy in improving their lives and leaving them better off whenever their paths crossed. For example, in his interaction with the Samaritan woman at the Well, despite being hungry, Jesus focused on drawing her into the Kingdom. Love superseded all tiredness and hunger, overrode the biases of the day, and the woman left the encounter having been affirmed of God's love for her and also set on her path to preach the gospel of the kingdom to everyone in her town (effectively becoming the first female evangelist) John 4:31-34.

True leaders want God's will at all costs. Whether in business, churches, organizations, or personally, your mission must be fuelled by the desire to improve lives and see people turn to God.

Jesus met needs: John 6:5

> 'Then Jesus lifted up His eyes, and seeing a great multitude coming toward Him, He said to Philip, "Where shall we buy bread, that these may eat?"'

Perceiving and meeting needs was vital to Jesus' mode of operation and success. We see repeated occurrences as the Scriptures continually reference his desire and the ability to meet needs.

The leader's job is to meet the needs of family, friends, team, followers, customers, or even mentors. As the saying goes, 'People don't care how much you know until they know how much you care.' Leaders rarely reach or influence people without meeting their needs.

Jesus was motivated by compassion

Leaders can create amazing change when motivated by compassion. Most people understand what it's like to be compelled to act by compassion: We see people hurting and want to help.

But Jesus is the compassion champion. Compassion messed up his plans, frustrated his followers, and threw his work-life balance out of whack. Right after John the Baptist's death, Jesus withdrew to a remote area (Matthew 14:13). So often surrounded by crowds,

> *'People don't care how much you know until they know how much you care.'*
> **- Theodore Roosevelt**

he wanted to be alone, but the crowds found out where he was going, followed him and pressed in around him, eager to have their own needs filled.

In that state, the last thing we need is to be confronted with other people's demands, but Jesus 'had compassion on [the crowds] and healed their sick' (Matthew 14:14, words in brackets mine). He set his needs aside to minister to others, not because he had to, but because compassion made him want to.

Back in 2005, a lady in her early twenties joined our church. She wanted to be involved in the choir, but we soon discovered that she was pregnant. She had been part of a previous church where she became a Christian. Because she was not married, some of our congregation (not the leaders) raised objections along the lines of,

> 'Pastor, this lady has committed adultery/
> fornication/sexual relationship outside
> marriage! I don't think you should let her join
> the choir.'

> 'She shouldn't be allowed to join the choir; her sin will soon become evident.'

> 'What if someone enquires about this? We will be condoning the sin!'

I had to think about this for a while. As I did so, I realised what we needed was to show her compassion. My reply went this way:

> 'This girl moved to live alone in Kent from London, which probably means she's been rejected and feels embarrassed. For all you know, her family may have dissociated themselves from her. What if we are her last hope? Perhaps this is her way of looking for acceptance.'

> 'I don't want to be that pastor who turns her away because of sin and errors, when what she needs is someone to embrace and accept her.'

Once I worked that out, I decided to let her serve in the choir. The complaints started rolling in from different people, but I realised they were simply young in their understanding. We were between one and three years old as a church. And that kind of thinking was really more from the immature Christians. I didn't really mind because my compassion for her overrode this. We embraced her, she returned to school, eventually travelled abroad, and is now doing very well.

Compassion is an intrinsic leadership component. You must learn to love to lead effectively.

Jesus values everyone

You may have experienced the type of leader who surrounds himself with influential people, hoping to rise to their level. Hanging out with smart, beautiful, rich people may be a good strategy for worldly influencers, but not for Jesus. He sought out the ostracized, poor, sick, weak and rejected, those society deemed worthless.

Zacchaeus is a beautiful example (Luke 19). Zacchaeus was a despised tax collector working for the Roman government. His height prevented him from seeing Jesus through the crowds, so he climbed up a tree. Based on his reputation, Jesus could have justifiably walked on by, but instead, the Lord spotted Zacchaeus on the tree, called him by name and offered to visit his home. Zacchaeus' life changed from that moment. He repented of his sin and determined to share his wealth.

That's the power of being valued by Jesus.

2. HUMILITY

> Since God chose you to be the holy people he
> loves, you must clothe yourselves with tender-

> hearted mercy, kindness, humility,
> gentleness, and patience.
> — Colossians 3:12 (NLT)

There are 'know-it-all' and 'submit-or-else' leaders who may appear successful, but Proverbs 16:5 calls the proud 'an abomination' to God. Pride and arrogance do not model or demonstrate Christ's interests. They are in direct conflict with Christian leadership.

It is easy to isolate ourselves in a bubble of self-knowledge and self-assurance, kicking out opinions that do not align with ours. But the result is often prideful and being addicted to the power and authority associated with leadership.

Humility flows out of proper perspective and a grateful heart. The humble leader gives Christ his rightful place as Lord, understanding that not everything depends on her and that everything is possible with God. She is grateful for who God is, for his costly salvation plan and for the gifts, talents, business opportunities, and significant purpose God has provided. Secure in her identity in Christ and humbly aware of her strengths, she willingly admits her weaknesses and mistakes, invites dissenting opinions and freely gives credit and recognition. She also places the right people in the right roles with the freedom to perform.

Jesus had a servant's heart: Matthew 20:28

> '…Just as the Son of Man did not come to
> be served, but to serve, and to give His life a
> ransom for many.'

Jesus focused on serving his disciples' and followers' needs without an attitude of entitlement. In addition, instead of being 'untouchable', he was always found among those he served.

Leaders are servants.

(More on humility in Chapter Six)

3. DEVELOPMENT AND MOTIVATION

Jesus modelled self-development by moving away from the crowd to spend time alone with God, the most striking example being in Gethsemane just before His arrest. Jesus knew 'all things that would come upon Him' (John 18:4), including the painful flogging and crucifixion, causing him intense anguish and sorrow:

> 'And He was withdrawn from them about a
> stone's throw, and He knelt down and prayed,
> saying, 'Father, if it is Your will, take this cup
> away from Me; nevertheless, not My will, but
> Yours, be done.' Then an angel appeared to Him
> from heaven, strengthening Him. And being
> in agony, He prayed more earnestly. Then His

sweat became like great drops of blood falling down to the ground.' Luke 22:41-44

Christian leaders should seek God for insight into His will and for strength and spiritual growth. Becoming more righteous is a lifelong process.

Jesus had a team: John 5:30

'I can of myself do nothing.'

Jesus couldn't accomplish much without a team, so he recruited twelve disciples who partnered with Him in spreading the Gospel. We were not meant to live or work alone. A team helps us fulfil our mission at the highest level. Without this, we are limited in what we can accomplish.

Motivation

Good leaders motivate instead of misleading and exploiting people. Nehemiah fearlessly motivated God's people to rebuild the walls of Jerusalem (Nehemiah 2:17). He laid out the vision and plan, reassuring them that God was with them. Moving people for our benefit can lead to manipulation and exploitation; however, in calling them to a higher purpose – God's will – we motivate them.

In Matthew 28:19-20, just as he was leaving the earth, Jesus instructed his disciples to continue with the mission – to disciple the nations. Then, he further promised to equip them with the Holy Spirit's anointing (Acts 1:8).

Jesus empowered people: Luke 10:19

> 'Behold, I give you the authority to trample on serpents and scorpions and over all the power of the enemy, and nothing shall by any means hurt you.'

Jesus empowered those around him to fulfil his mission. The global movement we are experiencing today would not reach its full potential without people empowered for the assignment.

Empower those around you to operate in their personal strengths for the greatest impact and long-term success.

> *'God's call on my life has been driven, orchestrated, and identified in the place of prayer, established and backed by the written Word (the Bible) and then confirmed through prophetic words received from people like Pastor Eddie. He played a pivotal role in my realising certain assignments by entrusting certain church departments and ministries to me. This appointment served as practical platforms to coach, mentor and bring theoretical leadership topics and teachings to life. Pastor Eddie had noticed in my first month of meeting him (20 years ago) that I learn better and faster by observation. If I see it done once, I will replicate it. So, he helped me grow in this direction.*
> *— Tunde Adeboga*

Jesus made good use of His time: Luke 5:16

> 'So, He Himself often withdrew into the
> wilderness and prayed.'

Jesus intentionally balanced his time alone and with others, scheduling time alone to regroup, recharge, rest and unwind, and time to be around others to grow, fellowship, and serve. He was never reactive with His time, whether alone or with others.

To avoid burnout, it is critical to pace yourself, value and balance the time between you and God and then with those you serve. The effective Christian leader maintains an ongoing, personal, intimate relationship with God through practices like prayer, fasting and carving out the time to hear from God. When we are intentional, we become proactive.

Jesus Always Speaks the Truth

Jesus called the Pharisees a 'brood of vipers' a few times (Matthew 3:7, 12:34, 23:33). These men had great religious influence, but Jesus was more concerned with sharing His message, not gaining political support. Conversely, he did not use hard-hitting truths to rile the people already on his side. Whether or not it was to his advantage and at the cost of his supporters, he spoke the truth. The undiluted truth sets us free, so let us pray that our current and future leaders will courageously speak the truth with love, even when it might be costly.

Correction versus Forgiveness

Appropriately correcting others is essential. Many Scripture verses speak to this principle, as the following examples illustrate:

- 'And let us consider one another in order to stir up love and good works, not forsaking the assembling of ourselves together, as is the manner of some, but exhorting one another, and so much the more as you see the Day approaching' (Hebrews 10:24-25).

- And we urge you, brethren, to recognize those who labour among you, and are over you in the Lord and admonish you, and to esteem them very highly in love for their work's sake. Be at peace among yourselves. Now we exhort you, brethren, warn those who are unruly, comfort the fainthearted, uphold the weak, be patient with all' (1 Thessalonians 5:13-14).

- 'But avoid foolish and ignorant disputes, knowing that they generate strife. And a servant of the Lord must not quarrel

but be gentle to all, able to teach, patient,
in humility correcting those who are
in opposition, if God perhaps will grant
them repentance, so that they may know
the truth, and that they may come to
their senses and escape the snare of the
devil, having been taken captive by him
to do his will' (2 Timothy 2:23-26).

The Christian leader can approach matters of correction using the following suggestions:

- Understand the individual's temperament and be patient as necessary.

- Respect their concerns and opinions. Patiently explain why things may not go as planned.

- Allow them to express their God-given gifts and ability as appropriate.

- Support their dreams with step-by-step guidance towards actualisation.

- Challenge their flaws in love, presenting appropriate ways or steps that could have been taken.

Jesus was forgiving: John 21:15-19

"So, when they had eaten breakfast, Jesus said to Simon Peter, 'Simon, son of Jonah, do you love Me more than these?' He said to Him, 'Yes, Lord; You know that I love You.' He said to him, 'Feed My lambs.' He said to him again a second time, 'Simon, son of Jonah, do you love Me?' He said to Him, 'Yes, Lord; You know that I love You.' He said to him, 'Tend My sheep.' He said to him the third time, 'Simon, son of Jonah, do you love Me?' Peter was grieved because He said to him the third time, 'Do you love Me?' And he said to Him, 'Lord, You know all things; You know that I love You.'

'Jesus said to him, 'Feed My sheep. Most assuredly, I say to you, when you were younger, you girded yourself and walked where you wished; but when you are old, you will stretch out your hands, and another will gird you and carry you where you do not wish.' This He spoke, signifying by what death he would glorify God. And when He had spoken this, He said to him, 'Follow Me.'"

After Peter's denial, Jesus meets with Peter privately after the resurrection in a remarkable demonstration of grace, forgiveness, and great love.

Forgiveness is an attitude. Everyone makes mistakes, and Jesus understood that quickly forgiving allowed for a happier life and being closer to those around him. Because he understood that people are human, he was always quick to forgive.

A young man approached me many years ago, asking me for mentorship. He even went as far as calling himself my 'Elisha'[1]. The opportunity to add value to this young man's life was exciting. Then he told me he had nowhere to live, so I invited him to stay with my family. After a while, it dawned on me that he had been asking for financial assistance in one form or the other. At first, I gladly obliged as his 'mentor', but then, one day, he disappeared without warning. He wouldn't return my calls and I could not get hold of him. At first, I thought it was something I had done wrong. I was sad that a relationship I had invested so much in would suddenly end like this. This feeling was followed by my realising I had inadvertently exposed my family to a scammer. My rush of emotions was palpable. I questioned my judgment in granting this individual access into our lives. I repeatedly processed where I went wrong. Shock, grief and anger played on my mind continually until I had to put a stop to it all by deciding to forgive him.

---

1   Elijah's successor in the Bible. Their mentoring relationship is a remarkable study.

In Matthew 18, Peter, trying to be generous, asks Jesus if forgiving someone 'up to seven times' (Matthew 18:21) is sufficient. To his shock, Jesus says he needs to forgive 'seventy times seven' times (Matthew 18:22). However much we think we should forgive; we can do more. Jesus doesn't forgive because it's socially acceptable, but to set people free. He doesn't want anything blocking our access to life in all its fullness (John 10:10).

Great leaders understand the power of forgiveness and understanding. Granting grace and prompt forgiveness keeps us happier and breeds loyalty and productivity as we strive toward our goals.

Let's value leaders who willingly forgive, forgive them when required, and not hold grudges that grow into bitterness.

4. INTEGRITY

> 'Righteous lips are the delight of kings,
> and they love him who speaks what is right.'
> - Proverbs 16:13

Integrity entails practising what we preach, being consistent and dependable, doing what we say we will do and being trustworthy.

'To do what is right and just is more acceptable
to the Lord than sacrifice.' - Proverbs 21:3

Integrity is the foundation on which all other leadership qualities are built. Proverbs 21:3 reminds us of Jesus' call for our actions to reflect our faith, righteousness and justice. Servant leaders do not cheat, lie, and manipulate, but we are to be different, countercultural and honest. The world says to do whatever it takes to achieve success, books advise us to dress and act in certain ways to get noticed, and fairy tales are all about believing in ourselves. But Jesus' way is humility and integrity.

Integrity is a lifestyle with an overall track record of honesty and good repute. We may stumble and fall short now and again (because we are human), but we confess those faults before God and those we lead. Living with integrity, especially in the face of challenges and temptations, is an incredible witness to those we mentor.

Many over-simplify integrity and miss the significance of this quality for the Christian Leader. Integrity is multidimensional. Empowered by the Holy Spirit, it occurs in complete alignment with God's will and requires courageous self-discipline.

5. HONESTY

Honesty is a critical sub-trait of integrity that deserves to be highlighted. There is no twilight zone with honesty—a thing is right or wrong, black or white. Today, we hide dishonesty behind euphemisms like 'grey areas,' 'half-truths,' or 'little white lies.'

Honesty begins with us. People are experts at lying and self-deceit, but dishonesty is usually easy to spot and detrimental to an organization or church. Without honesty, trust is lost, and relationships suffer.

6. FOLLOWER OF GOD'S WILL

Paul says: 'Imitate me, just as I also imitate Christ' (1 Corinthians 11:1, NKJV). Nothing is more important than for a leader to seek God's direction, commit his way to him, and count on him to establish the next steps.

7. SUBMISSIVENESS AND SERVITUDE

Jesus was a model servant to the Father.

> 'He died for everyone so that those who receive
> his new life will no longer live for themselves.
> Instead, they will live for Christ, who died and
> was raised for them'
> (2 Corinthians 5:15).

Being a servant-leader requires being humble and secure in our identity and caring for those we serve. Yes, we strive to serve the people with excellence, deliver value and be a blessing in every interaction, but in seeking men's approval over God's, we cling to position, power, and authority for ego's sake.

In Matthew 20:25-28, Jesus says this about leadership:

> 'But Jesus called them together and said, 'You know that the rulers in this world lord it over their people, and officials flaunt their authority over those under them. But among you, it will be different. Whoever wants to be a leader among you must be your servant, and whoever wants to be first among you must become your slave. For even the Son of Man came not to be served but to serve others and to give his life as a ransom for many.''

Our goal in Christ is not to grab power or make our names known. We are to make God's name known, love and respect the people in our care, and use the authority we have been given with grace.

8. OBEDIENCE

The obedient leader lives for an audience of One. As a wise and faithful steward, he applies God's principles to everyday business decisions. He pursues holiness and practices self- discipline by doing the right thing, whether or not he feels like it. Leaders must lead themselves first through discipline; then, they can focus on leading others. Many get this out of order, and weak character sabotages their success.

9. FAITHFULNESS

The two main components of faithfulness are living by faith and being trustworthy. Living by faith means seeking and trusting God, pursuing the mission He's given us with courage, taking risks, and persevering through difficult times. We rest on His character, rely on His promises, and do things His way.

The faithful Christian Leader also seeks to be a person God can trust - recognizing that God leads and has entrusted everything to His followers. He is answerable to God in work, relationships, lifestyle and more, and looks forward with hope and joy to the day he stands before the Lord to hear: 'Well done, good and faithful servant!'

We can see all these principles in Jesus and learn from him. Jesus came from a small town and partnered with twelve people to spread a movement that transcended centuries. Needless to say, Jesus was a remarkable leader on Earth and can teach us a thing or two about being a leader of significance.

May we be empowered to live according to the example of the greatest leader of all time, Jesus.

Who is a Christian Leader?

THE QUALIFIED LEADER

1. A leader honours and submits to God's authority.
From Genesis to Revelation, the Bible contrasts leaders who honoured God with loving obedience with those who honoured themselves. People prospered under leaders who honoured and sought after God but were oppressed by leaders who did not.

God's first two commandments to Israel in Exodus 20:3- 4 were to have no other gods before Him and not to make any image for the purpose of worship. Today, we revere and honour those in leadership roles, sometimes more than the Lord.

With leadership often comes recognition and the temptation to put ourselves or our status before God, and if we're not careful, we can worship the position instead of the One who promoted us there.

2 A leader knows and cares for their people.

Good leaders are like shepherds, caring for and watching over the people entrusted to them (1 Peter 5:1-5). This reference to shepherds may not mean a lot to us today, but it perfectly describes the godly leader. A shepherd knew each sheep, named and cared for them, inspected their health and taught them his voice. If one wandered away, the shepherd didn't forget about it or merely hope it would come back. He went out, found and brought it back to the flock.

Likewise, the leader should regularly communicate with his people. He should ask genuine, caring questions and do all he can to serve his team. Good leaders motivate and mobilize others to accomplish tasks with creativity, vision, integrity, and skill, investing in their development and well-being for the common good.

3. A leader can be of any age.
In 1 Timothy 4:12, Paul tells young pastor Timothy, 'Don't let anyone look down on you because you are young, but set an example for the believers in speech, in conduct, in love, in faith, and in purity.'

From the above, we see that what qualifies this leader is not how young, old, experienced, or inexperienced she is. Just because a potential (or actual) leader is younger doesn't make them less capable. Instead, the qualification is based on how they conduct themselves, their relationship with God, their moral standing, and an ability to encourage with their actions and words.

*Ministry Leadership was not
something I considered or thought I was gifted
to do. I wanted to serve behind the scenes, but Pastor
Eddie identified and gradually nurtured my gift, from
being placed in a small men's leadership group to
planning events in small committees. My self-discovery
journey was initially infused with doubts. Can I do this?
Am I making an impact? Then the testimonies
started coming in as people expressed how
they were being blessed.*

*The most helpful thing for me was connecting with the
people. I realised early on that Pastor Eddie is
not removed from the people. Instead, he has varying
degrees of close relationships that cut across different
demographics. I adopted the same approach, which
naturally draws people and makes leadership easier.
This could be challenging when some see you as the
person and not the leader, unlike the business setting
where your job title does the groundwork.*

*The sky becomes the limit as other unrelated
departments seek my counsel, friends and colleagues
request mentorship, and relatives ask for advice on
different aspects of life. I have no expertise, just
grace. I leave the house everyday wanting to give
more, be more than I was yesterday,
earn more, and help more.*
— *Kayode Suulola*

This biblical list helps determine what to look for and how to avoid pride and arrogance, ageism and similar pitfalls.

4. A leader is someone you want to follow

In a paraphrase of Proverbs 29:2, The Message says, 'When good people run things, everyone is glad, but when the ruler is bad, everyone groans.'

You can feel the excitement and hope for progress if the leader is someone you want to follow. But what about when that's not the case? How do you respond to leadership that is the total opposite of the godly leader?

In 1 Timothy 2, Paul tells us to 'pray for kings and all those in authority, that we may live peaceful and quiet lives in all godliness and holiness.' This wasn't pie- in-the-sky thinking. Paul wrote these words under one of the harshest rulers in history, Emperor Nero, who was worse than any leader today. We can pray for our leaders to have the wisdom to discern how best to lead and for unity within the organization. Don't tear down or degrade your leader. Lift him up to God, the only one who can help.

CHAPTER TWO

THE LEADERSHIP STYLES OF JESUS

'When Jesus heard it, He departed from there by boat to a deserted place by Himself. But when the multitudes heard it, they followed Him on foot from the cities. And when Jesus went out, He saw a great multitude; and He was moved with compassion for them and healed their sick.

When it was evening, His disciples came to Him, saying, 'This is a deserted place, and the hour is already late. Send the multitudes away, that they may go into the villages and buy themselves food.'

But Jesus said to them, 'They do not need to go away. You give them something to eat.'

And they said to Him, 'We have here only five loaves and two fish.'

He said, 'Bring them here to Me.'

Then, He commanded the multitudes to sit down on the grass. And He took the five loaves and the two fish, and looking up to heaven, He blessed and broke and gave the loaves to the disciples; and the disciples gave to the multitudes. So, they all ate and were filled, and they took up twelve baskets full of the fragments that remained. Now those who had eaten were about five thousand men, besides women and children' Matthew 14:13-21 NKJV.

Jesus models four leadership traits worth emulating in this account:

1. HE WAS WILLING TO BE INTERRUPTED

The story starts off with Jesus desiring to be alone after hearing about John the Baptist's tragic death, which seems like a fair request. His cousin had been brutally murdered, and all Jesus wanted was to not be bothered for a while. However, the crowds followed him. Rather than becoming angry or frustrated, Jesus compassionately healed all their sick, and the interruption turned out to be an even greater ministry opportunity to feed 5000 men (not counting women and children) with five loaves and two fishes.

There will often be people in need when we already have our own plans, but we must recognise that life's interruptions can be God-sent movements as part of his work.

2. HE WILLINGLY DID THE WORK

Jesus had been healing the sick and teaching until late in the evening, and the crowds became hungry. The disciples suggested sending them away before they had a mob on their hands.

Jesus replied, 'You give them something to eat (v 16).'

Concern for the crowd's dinner plans was probably not on the agenda for that day (especially since they had barged into his private mourning space). But Jesus didn't deflect the problem. He took responsibility for solving a mammoth, near-impossible task for any group of human beings to fulfil, let alone twelve disciples. Once the provision arrived, he personally supervised the distribution right up to collecting the leftovers afterwards.

Having an overall responsibility does not translate to being too good for mundane tasks. Every leader should joyfully do whatever the kingdom of God requires. Leaders lead by example and through service and, as Jesus did, get into the trenches and do the work with their followers.

3. JESUS BROUGHT OTHERS ALONG

Despite His willingness to do the work, Jesus did not attempt to do everything on His own. He trained and developed those around him. When the only solution the disciples could find was to send the crowds away, Jesus challenged them to do something greater to stretch and strengthen them.

Are we developing the potential leaders around us? Do we take the time to empower them to participate in our ongoing ministry? Can we be more patient with those under our leadership to help them dream and see that God may be up to something bigger than they can imagine?

A gentleman had been part of our church since day one. Once I identified that he was ready to move towards leadership, I asked if he would take the announcements one Sunday. He agreed. Without asking him, I know he would have rehearsed those few minutes repeatedly before the day. After the first time, his humorous delivery had the church in stitches, and he naturally started adding stories to his announcements. Soon, he wrote his first book, went into public speaking, and became an MC at functions.

Just like Jesus in that situation, we cannot do everything, even if we so desire. Jesus was willing and ready to build up leaders around Him. We should be doing the same.

4. JESUS DID WHAT OTHERS COULD NOT

Jesus gives leaders a pattern to follow. He was willing to do the work, bring others along, and, when they couldn't quite come through, do what they could not. When all the disciples could scrounge up was a meagre five loaves of bread and two fish, Jesus did the impossible and multiplied the food. He did not rebuke the disciples for not finding enough food or coming up with a better plan. He honoured their genuine effort.

Just like Jesus, excellent leaders graciously pick up the slack where plans fall short. There is no need for harsh rebukes or stern lectures that make people feel less valuable. We should recognise their honest and deliberate efforts and be willing to accomplish what they could not.

Emulating Jesus makes a leader worth following. It may take time, effort, and additional energy that we would rather not exert, but when we allow ourselves to be led by Jesus, we accomplish more than we ever thought possible.

Not knowing where I fit after joining our church, I volunteered in several departments. Pastor Eddie soon identified my organisational and people skills, and with his guidance, training, and mentorship, I progressed from leading the outreach team, men's ministry, and church operations, to pastoring one of the campus teams.

As ministers of the gospel, much of what we do is caught rather than taught. I learned much from observing Pastor Eddie's leadership styles, which helped me apply my gifting within the workforce, shadow learning along the way, while leading and steering volunteers towards positive outcomes.

I frequently struggled with juggling my day job and ministry, but Pastor Eddie regularly challenged me to take on strategic responsibilities to move the ministry forward, while growing as a leader in the marketplace.

Pastor Eddie's Be More, Do More, Give More and Build Better taught me and my colleagues to be versatile problem solvers.

The opportunity arose for me to lead the Medway campus, a significant responsibility that pushed me beyond where I was comfortable. Pastor Eddie's 1-1 mentoring and guidance in this role stretched my leadership capacity in the following areas:

- *Pastoring a campus*
- *Strategic leadership for campus growth*
- *Building and leading volunteers.*
- *Building human capital and a team of leaders.*

— *John T Ogbe*

We can look to Jesus for examples of wise, loving leadership, but he is so different from the majority of earthly leaders that it seems foolish to compare them, especially when the more important comparison is between us and Jesus. Are we speaking the truth? Giving Jesus our whole hearts? Valuing others? Acting with compassion and forgiving more often than we would like?

5. JESUS ASKS FOR AND OFFERS MORE

I was in full time employment when we started Gateway Chapel in a job that required me to travel around Europe. To ensure that I modelled the right example, I was always the first to arrive in church and the last to leave, even when I was travelling for work. In practice, that meant that I would often travel straight from the airport to church on a Friday evening. The result was that I did not have to harass the members of the church to commit to anything. They learned from

> *Pastor Eddie expects the same level of excellence at church that we demonstrate at work, and he has shared several testimonies about being in our position. Every leader is encouraged to submit and give our best, knowing that the vision's fulfilment depends on God's empowerment.*
> **- Bukky Kumolu-Johnson**

watching me and today, we have high commitment levels from leaders and volunteers.

While Jesus' yoke is easy and his burden light (Matthew 11:30), his plan has a steep joining fee. He says, 'Whoever wants to be my disciple must deny themselves and take up their cross and follow me' (Matthew 16:24).

'Take up your cross' would be a horrible campaign slogan. No one would go for it. But Jesus was playing the long game—for eternity. The journey may be rough, but he reminds us that it's worth it: 'What good is it for someone to gain the whole world, and yet lose or forfeit their very self?' (Luke 9:25). Jesus offers us an eternity full of joy with him, but not in exchange for a percentage of our hearts. He wants our hearts, souls, minds, and strength (Mark 12:30). May our commitment to Jesus be far greater than our commitment to earthly leaders, even when following him is difficult.

6. JESUS VALUES US MORE

Why would Jesus ask us to deny ourselves and follow him? Because that's what it takes to have a relationship with him. Jesus is not a political candidate who needs our support; he wants our company. He wants to enjoy life with us, starting here on Earth and continuing into eternity. No earthly leader can match this offer.

Jesus paid our debt of sin with his death: '...For the joy set before him he endured the cross, scorning its shame....' (Hebrews 12:2). The joy of fellowship with us was greater than the pain of the Cross. And he didn't stop there! He's still seeking and calling us. His relentless, unstoppable love for humanity should guide and direct our interactions with one another.

7. COMPARING JESUS AND JOHN'S LEADERSHIP STYLES

Let's examine Matthew 11:18-19 (KJV):

> 'For John came neither eating nor drinking,
> and they say, He hath a devil. The Son of man
> came eating and drinking, and they say, Behold
> a man gluttonous, and a winebibber, a friend of
> publicans and sinners. But wisdom is justified of
> her children.'

John was your tough legalistic accuser and righteous law upholder who reminded everyone to repent and be baptized or face God's wrath. John bluntly confronted sin with an aggressiveness that served a purpose in his day and may well be needed to tackle evil in certain people, sins, and situations.

Besides this rough confrontational style, John was sincerely holy and loved God's righteousness. However, telling King Herod that God would punish him for taking his brother's wife cost John his head!

Jesus, on the other hand, was usually a tender-hearted mercy-giver. When the people caught the woman in the act of adultery, did he say,

'Okay, let God's judgments rain down, stone her!' No. Instead, he told her to go and sin no more, teaching us that no one is worthy or holy enough to condemn another. Everyone can repent, be forgiven, and start a new life within God's will.

Jesus was not usually confrontational, except with false religious teachers, whom he referred to as hypocrites. His classic way was to offer forgiveness while subliminally rebuking and exposing hypocrisy through the Holy Spirit's conviction.

So, John attacks and condemns with the truth, but Jesus loves and forgives with the truth. Does this remind you of people you know? Some Christians accuse their leaders and everyone else of this and that. They are hard, harsh, and unforgiving, while others offer understanding and forgiveness.

When someone sins within the Church, certain individuals will throw stones, asking the pastor to confront, condemn, attack, and beat the person with the truth. You will hear complaints like,

'The pastor is not rebuking the sinners!'

'The leaders are not doing their job!'

However, the pastors may be unaware of the sins. People are good at hiding and covering up, and in addition, the stories may not be the whole truth. When we allow the Holy Spirit to work in people, he will teach us when to reject and rebuke or love and heal in each situation.

I once discovered a case of domestic abuse where the husband habitually hit his wife, so I decided to visit the family. On my arrival, he reacted immediately

'Pastor, I know exactly what you are going to say,' He muttered, before reeling off a few relevant Scriptures.

'Why am I here if you already know all this?' I asked him. 'Knowledge is useless unless we act on it.' Thankfully, the Holy Spirit gave us the right approach in handling the situation. They are still married today, so he must have changed his approach.

Confrontational people do not care if the person being accused gets offended and lost from God and the church. They just want action taken against the 'sinful' person and to be deemed a great leader for tackling the situation. While this makes them feel righteous, it amounts to spiritual pride. Unless there is evidence of damaging sin, this is not good for the Church. It also detracts from sins they should be working on. Consider these verses:

> 'Therefore, strengthen your feeble arms and weak knees. 'Make level paths for your feet,' so that the lame may not be disabled, but rather healed. Make every effort to live in peace with all men and to be holy; without holiness no one will see the Lord.'
> - Hebrews 12:12-15 (NIV)

In the battle to gain souls for the Kingdom of God, we are continually tested in these areas. A principle to live by when sin is exposed in someone else is to examine our hearts in case we have erred. Many people often end up crossing the same bridge as those they condemn.

Are you focusing more on others' sins than yours? Do you want their faults dealt with harshly, knowing you would never tolerate your own medicine? God is calling us to higher levels of service, and it is always better to err on the side of mercy than judgment.

> 'For with what judgment ye judge, ye shall be judged: and with what measure ye mete, it shall be measured to you again.' - Matthew 7:2

Have you wronged or sinned against anyone? Now is the time to come clean. Even if you confess something you think the other person should also be confessing to, leave it to God. He knows how to deal with them. For all you know, they may have talked to him about it.

More importantly, how will God judge you?

Work on your character

Here is some counsel on dealing with your own character to offer healing, forgiveness, and a new start for those who seem to not deserve it:

> 'But exhort one another daily, while it is called today; lest any of you be hardened through the deceitfulness of sin.' - Hebrews 3:13

> 'Confess your faults one to another, and pray one for another, that ye may be healed. The effectual fervent prayer of a righteous man availeth much.' James 5:16

We offer forgiveness and deal with exposed sins by encouraging and praying for one another. And the time to do so is now to avoid becoming deeply bitter, stop worshipping and serving, and ultimately walk away from God. You need Christian friends to point out your faults from God's word from time to time.

That said, going back to the lady who joined our choir, my first consideration was that we are human and frail. This is why salvation is by grace, not works. God understands our humanity more than most. Secondly, I recognised that she needed restoration. The Bible says to restore, not condemn the lost brother (Galatians 6:1).

Some considered John crazy for abstaining from wine and eating locusts, but when Jesus drank wine and mixed with publicans, that disqualified and made him unholy. But who is accusing whom and why? Those condemning others are often guilty of the same sins. Drinking or not drinking wine was not the issue. Most people (especially the unspiritual carnal crowd) will never be happy with what the leader or righteous Christian does, whether he is harsh or soft, a rebuker, or a healer.

Jesus and John lost their lives to the envy and discomfort of evil hearts convicted of sin. On close examination, many men and women of God carry spiritual power and authority that, by words or good deeds, exposes sin for what it is, and people react differently to this righteous authority.

Let's look at four different reactions:

1. Those who respect and submit to the Word. These good sheep, like John the Beloved, make the Lord happy by their submission and obedience. They want sin out of their lives, and by allowing God to expose it during prayer, they become

authentic Christians able to lead and teach.

> 'Most men will proclaim every one his own goodness: but a faithful man who can find?' - Proverbs 20:6

2. Those who want to be first. Do you recall how James and John and their mother argued with others about who would have the most power in heaven? (Mark 10:36) What kind of a manipulating mother was that?

   Some people want to dominate others and be first. They usually want the title and honour without the responsibilities. But Jesus said the first are last, and the greatest should be the servant. Could this power-seeking person be you?

3. The deceptive ones. These followers tend to have personal agendas. Judas wanted Jesus to help the Jews obtain power over the Romans. He followed but was not 'one' with or supporting Jesus' soul-winning mission. Whenever Judas didn't like something, he objected vigorously. When Mary Magdalene washed Jesus' feet with oil, Judas wanted to demonstrate that he was more compassionate than the others. And

when he didn't get what he wanted from Jesus, Judas eventually betrayed him. Could this ulterior motive-driven person be you?

4. The non-committed distant followers - They follow no leader for very long. At one time, there were more than seventy disciples. Then Jesus gave a hard sermon, and the number shrunk to twelve. These comfortable Christians go so far and no further. They are unwilling to go all the way.

> 'And he said, Therefore, said I unto you, that no man can come unto me, except it were given unto him of my Father. From that time, many of his disciples went back, and walked no more with him. Then said Jesus unto the twelve, Will ye also go away? Then Simon Peter answered him, Lord, to whom shall we go? thou hast the words of eternal life.' - John 6:65-68 (KJV)

This category of people often leaves or shops from church to church, refusing to commit or submit to anyone. These misguided Christians are not obeying or doing any work for Jesus. They want God's blessings without sending saved souls to the Bank of Heaven, so their value to God is deficient.

Which are you? The submitted follower? The power-tripping challenger? The deceptive manipulator? Or the too-comfortable non-committed doing little to win souls for Jesus? It is easy to look good to people, but God knows our hearts.

Are you following Jesus for power, your agenda, or comfort? Submit and be willing to die for our Lord. God knows where you stand on your journey to being a real leader. The paradox is that submission and belonging to Jesus equals real freedom. Lead others as you follow, not letting your plans remain your own. Remember, only what is done for Jesus has a lasting legacy.

For the Christian leader, character is the moral and ethical foundation for the kind of success that honours God.

CHAPTER THREE

SERVANT LEADERSHIP

WHAT IS SERVANT-LEADERSHIP?

'Whoever would be first among you must be the servant of all' (Mk 10:42-44; Mt 20:25-28).

Jesus expected his followers' practices to be distinctly different from the world's self-seeking, self-serving, and domineering leadership style.

Servant-leadership in Practice

Within the servant-leadership framework, everyone works to the same end based on their expertise and assignment rather than being positioned by rank or title. Each team member playing a meaningful leadership role generates a receptive climate and infectious energy.

Servant-leadership does not negate accountability or responsibility, either. The role may require applying correction or appropriate discipline to maintain the community's integrity to its statement of faith, standards, core values, and accepted strategic goals.

A biblical base for understanding leadership

> 'Do nothing out of selfish ambition or vain conceit, but in humility consider others better than yourselves. Each of you should look not only to your own interests but also to the interests of others.' (Philippians 2:3-4)

God wants leaders who will listen to His will and execute it faithfully with divinely appointed authority.

Moses was the first to practice servant-leadership (Exodus 32:11-14, 30-35). Servant leaders strengthen the weak, empower those entrusted to their care, and also show compassion towards the disadvantaged and the lost (Ezekiel 34:2-10).

JESUS, THE ULTIMATE SERVANT-LEADER

When James and John asked Jesus to grant them leadership positions in his kingdom, Jesus warned them not to model their leadership philosophy on that of the 'Gentiles' and 'great men' of the world:

'Whoever would be first among you must be servant of all.' (Mark 10:42-44; Matthew 20:25-28)

The one who rules should be like the one who serves (Luke 22:26 ESV). Greatness in God's sight is not found in how many people serve the leader but how faithfully she serves. A relationship of mutual stimulation and investment converts followers into leaders, while the leader never fails to understand what it means to be a follower.

In John 13:1-17, Jesus gives a practical example of what it means to serve others. He washed his followers' feet, which was the house servant's responsibility. The passage shows that:

1. Jesus' basic motivation was love for his followers (v. 1).

2. Jesus was fully aware of his position as leader (v. 14). Before the disciples experienced him as their servant, he had long been their strong and extremely powerful leader and master.

3. Jesus voluntarily served his followers (v. 5-12). He did not come as their foot-washer but was ready to do this service if needed.

4. Jesus wanted to set an example for his disciples to follow (v. 14-15).

Jesus' washing his disciples' feet models the following:

- Having the right attitude is fundamental to servant-leadership. No one can lead effectively as a servant without first giving himself to leadership greater than his own. Jesus' life of service originated from his loving relationship and submission to the Father who sent him.

- Jesus served everyone, including Judas, who ultimately betrayed him. In washing his disciple's feet, he did not diminish but rather enhanced his position and influence as their teacher.

- Servant leadership translates values and dispositions into behaviour that serves without seeking external rewards. It frequently requires giving up personal rights and desires to serve God and others first.

- At heart, servant-leadership genuinely cares for others' well-being and does not use them for the leader's benefit or ignore them if they do not fit naturally into the leader's plans or vision.

Servant-leadership is not weak

Servant-leaders must first of all please God and are not moved by the need to please others:

> 'Am I now trying to win the approval of men,
> or of God? Or am I trying to please men? If I
> were still trying to please men, I would not be a
> servant of Christ.' (Gal 1:10)

Servant-leadership is not a model for the weak or for losers. A serving attitude does not imply a willingness to be abused or tolerate exploitation. It is not only about doing menial tasks or strategically satisfying the leader's own needs but also enabling others to do their best. The leader carries out every task with the larger vision in mind.

Servant-leaders graciously accept others who serve them as well as those who lead them. What distinguishes them is not necessarily the particular decision they make but their caring manner and their broad consultation in the process.

CHARACTERISTICS OF SERVANT-LEADERSHIP

Servant-leaders aspire to be great only in their service to others, serving with integrity, humility, sincere concern, a generous, forgiving and giving heart, and self-discipline. They invest in, empower, care for, and consult their team as a matter of course.

Servant-leadership involves direction, not aimless wandering, allowing elements of vision and process to work hand in hand. It cultivates:

- visionary, positive thinking and conceptualizing (the bigger picture)

- responsibility for commitment and a hunger for improvement

- development of moral, value-based leadership methods

- physical and intellectual vitality and fitness

- the capacity to achieve significant results

- service without expectation of reward

- appreciation and recognition for the strengths and work of others, and

- the ability to lead an enjoyable, balanced life.

The servant-leadership process 'walks the talk' by:

- seeking the common good as its primary motivation

- seeing work as a partnership of service in the community

- building a team spirit through shared and open decision-making

- developing a resilient and growing mind-set

- stewarding people and resources

- having a tolerance for people's mistakes as a redemptive learning process

- providing for life-long learning and

- holding the leader and others accountable.

Not all these qualities are found to the same degree in every leader, but great leaders recognise their strengths and weaknesses and surround themselves with people with complementary abilities.

Servant-leadership requires teamwork

Today's society regards openly dictatorial and self-serving leadership from the top down as socially unacceptable and ineffective. However, subtly camouflaged self-serving leadership still exists. Some organizations, including well-intentioned Christian ones, use a top-down, hierarchical leadership style, holding that the leader knows what is in their organization's best interests more than the people being served. They neglect enabling, consulting, and investing in others when the organization falters or is slow to produce desired results.

Serving from the heart is the best antidote to such abuse of power. It is better that leaders be wounded than that their followers suffer. No one is designated as the leader at all times. Roles shift as required for the team's activities, and titles are less important than functions as all stakeholders strive to work in harmony.

Servant-leadership and the authorities

All organizations require accountable authorities with the power to make the organization operational. Servant-leaders do not resist. They humbly submit to appropriate and godly authority as to the Lord.

SERVANT-LEADERSHIP AND DECISION-MAKING

Servant-leadership does not view decision-making from the leader's or even a team's perspective. Instead, it adopts a consultative and relational approach where many people think and act together throughout the entire process. Most policy decisions are made by those most affected by the decision or, at least, with their input, which the leaders facilitate and support to achieve organisational objectives through the collective effort. This approach engenders greater understanding and support across the organisation while discovering and developing prospective leaders.

Excellent leaders are accountable to those working above, level with, and below them (investing in the latter's development), and the process flows up, down and across the organization, capturing everyone's enthusiasm and loyalty. For all these reasons, servant-leadership works best when everyone in the organization is committed to the concept and understands the serving role of all responsible leaders, whatever their titles may be.

An emphasis on individual (and not primarily organizational) growth and potential distinguishes servant leadership from other leadership styles.

Just after commanding Christians to esteem others better than themselves, Paul said, 'Let this mind be in you, which was also in Christ Jesus' (Philippians 2:5). Christ repeatedly exemplified an attitude of service toward all within His reach.

God expects us to replace self-centeredness with concern for and a desire to see those we serve grow, advance and prosper. In yielding to God and the Holy Spirit, we embrace his heart, nature, and outlook, becoming kinder, more thoughtful, and compassionate, and service is a sheer joy and delight.

> *'True leadership must be for the benefit of the followers, not to enrich the leader.'*
> **— John C. Maxwell**

With this new disposition, the servant-leader finds that they genuinely care about others and intrinsically link mission success to individual success. 'True leadership must be for the benefit of the followers, not to enrich the leader. (Actors, 2019)' No matter the capacity you serve in, your success is not defined by your personal achievements but by those you influence.

Regardless of any achievement to date, we can always improve and impact more lives by adopting the servant leadership approach.

THE SERVANT LEADER

A servant leader is:

- A **Christ-centred voluntary** servant who is submitted to a higher purpose, far beyond his personal interests or the interests of others.

- A **leader** who serves others with the power entrusted to him.

- A **servant** who, out of love, serves others needs before his own.

- A **teacher** who **consistently** trains followers to become servant leaders themselves.

There is a big difference between serving the needs of others and being a servant of others' needs.

- **Serving the needs of others** is liberating. It implies recognizing their needs (without judging them) and then doing what can be done in line with the higher purpose of serving God first to help satisfy that need.

- **Being a servant of the needs of others** means doing anything and everything to satisfy those needs, whether it is in line with one's service to God or not.

- The servant leader is continually led and grown by the Holy Spirit.

- Servant leadership is more about being than about doing.

There are three dimensions in which Christian servant leaders must grow:

1. As a voluntary servant of God

2. As a servant of others, and

3. As a leader.

The committed servant needs to rightly employ their leadership gifts with love and without abusing their power. Leadership skills training, continuous encouragement and feedback can support a servant leader in this growth process.

Our growth track program made it easy to identify where I fit within the body, and through mentoring, I was able to become an effective leader.

Our support system was also helpful during my progression from member to volunteer to leader. I initially struggled with the concept that we are not all at the same stage in our Christian walk, and our level of service can vary, but I learned over time to pray about everything, providing mentorship and coaching as required.

Pastor Eddie's leadership significantly helped me in my career. Having worked in a leadership capacity in three key hospitality and entertainment organisations, I have stood out as a leader who cares and makes a difference.

In my first leadership role more than two decades ago, my style was based on what I decided was best and how I felt. My perspective has since changed, and I now pour time and care into those I lead. When you connect with and care for them, people feel appreciated and become more willing to do more and give more.

— Sarha Degnace

The average non-Christ-centred leader also needs training, encouragement, and feedback, but conversion to servanthood is a greater need, and this must be continuously reinforced. It is harder to serve than be served, especially for those in long-term senior leadership positions. Old habits die hard.

A servitude mindset doesn't occur through decision-making alone. It is first a gracious gift from God. Our new nature should readily draw us to the Christ-centred leadership style of our Role Model. How do you compare to Jesus' leadership model? Are you drawn to the higher purpose of serving God? Are you focused on helping those who follow you (remember, leaders have followers) achieve their full potential for the Kingdom? It takes intentionality to serve a higher purpose.

An interesting exercise is to read through Mark's Gospel for how Jesus led and developed that disparate collection of men who became his disciples and to whom he entrusted his Church. 'A servant leader sacrificially seeks the highest joy of those he serves[2].' So, determining whether or not a leader is acting from a heart of Christlike service is not simple and requires charitable, patient, and humble discernment. There's no one-size-fits-all servant leader description. The needs and contexts in the wider church are vast and varied and require many different kinds of leaders and gifts, so guarding against our biases

---

2   Robert Greenleaf

when assessing leaders' hearts is crucial. Everyone is drawn to certain kinds of leaders, but our preferences can be unreliable and unhelpful.

To identify true servant leadership requires following Christ's command and example. In Matthew 20 and 23, Christ tells us that we need, first of all, to lead with an attitude of servanthood.

> 'Yet it shall be not so among you but whoever desires to become great among you, let him be your servant. And whoever desires to be first among you, let him be your servant, just as the Son of Man did not come to be served, but to serve, and to give His life a ransom for many.'
> Matthew 20:26-28

> 'But he who is greatest among you shall be your servant.' Matthew 23:11

When the disciples disputed over who would be the greatest among them (Luke 9: 46-50; 22: 24-30; Mark 9: 33-37; 10: 35-45; Matthew 20: 20-28), they were preoccupied with positions of power and authority, measuring greatness in positional terms, which led to a 'power struggle' of sorts. Jesus offered himself as a paradigm for them to follow. Back to washing their feet, this job belonged to the lowest servant in a Jewish household, and none of Jesus' disciples, despite their dirty and dusty feet, chose the role. Instead, Jesus got up and gave them a practical demonstration of 'servant leadership'. It has recently been fashionable to talk or teach about this, but we need more people practising this style of leadership.

MARKS OF A SERVANT LEADER

Still, the New Testament instructs us to exercise due diligence in discerning a Christian leader's fitness (1 Timothy 3:1–13). What traits point to a Christlike orientation? Here are five fundamental indicators.

1. A servant leader seeks his master's glory

Jesus said, 'The one who speaks on his own authority seeks his own glory; but the one who seeks the glory of him who sent him is true, and in him there is no falsehood' (John 7:18). As Christ's bondservant (Ephesians 6:6) he demonstrates over time that Christ, not public approval, position, or financial security, has his primary loyalty. In this, he 'swears to his own hurt and does not change' (Psalm 15:4).

2. A servant leader sacrifices for those he serves

This does not conflict with the above point. Again, Jesus said, 'Whoever would be great among you must be your servant . . . even as the Son of Man came not to be served but to serve, and to give his life as a ransom for many' (Matthew 20:26, 28). Whatever his temperament, gift mix, capacity, or sphere of influence, he sacrifices to pursue their 'progress and joy in the faith,' which results in greater glory to God (Philippians 1:25; 2:9–11).

3. A servant leader will forgo his rights rather than obscure the gospel

'A servant leader's identity and trust are not in his calling, but in his Christ.'

Paul said it this way: 'I have made myself a servant to all, that I might win more of them' (1 Corinthians 9:19). This meant that he did things like abstaining from certain foods and drinks, refusing financial support, working to provide for himself, going hungry or homeless, and enduring disrespect (1 Corinthians 4:11–13; 9:4–7). He also decided against getting married (1 Corinthians 9:5), all of which amounted to yielding his rights to win more people to Christ.

4. A servant leader is not preoccupied with personal visibility and recognition

Like John the Baptist, a servant leader sees himself as a 'friend of the Bridegroom' (John 3:29) and is not preoccupied with visibility. He doesn't view those with less visible roles as less significant, nor does he covet more visible roles as more significant (1 Corinthians 12:12–26). He seeks to steward the role he's received as best he can and gladly leaves the role assignments to God (John 3:27).

5. A servant leader anticipates and graciously accepts the time for his decrease

Leaders are in place for a season, whether long, short, abundant or lean, recorded or not. But the seasons end, and as John the Baptist commented at the end of his season, 'Therefore this joy of mine is now complete. He must increase, but I must decrease' (John 3:29–30).

The leader or other people may be the first to recognize his season's end, and God may even allow an unjust ending for purposes he may not yet understand. None of this prevents him from graciously yielding to Christ's cause because his identity and trust are not in his calling.

To identify God's call on my life and where I fit within the body, I spent time listening to and closely observing Pastor Eddie. With the Holy Spirit's help, I gained much insight and understanding from his teachings. Also, the Holy Spirit often spoke to me while I was serving as God often uses circumstances and situations as illustrations. A key principle I learned was to accept that everyone is a work in progress. We judge no one since we are all like clay being shaped by the Potter.

For me, being Christlike amounts to serving others, sacrificial living and being kind at every opportunity.

*— **Bola Oso***

No earthly Christian leader perfectly depicts all five marks of servanthood, apart from Jesus. The majority are imperfect servants trying to be faithful.

So, some of the greatest gifts we can give our leaders are:

1) Explicit encouragement whenever we observe these graces in them (loosen our tongues),

2) Quiet patience if they stumble (hold our tongues) and

3) Give gracious feedback about decisions, questions, and concerns (bridle our tongues).

We can easily apply all three while speaking about or to our leaders. If a leader needs help realising his season is ending, his faithful friends should bring loving, gracious, gentle, and patient encouragement and, if needed, reproof.

CHAPTER FOUR

SERVANT LEADERSHIP IN NEHEMIAH

Nehemiah's life is a wonderful model for the modern-day leader. Upon learning that his people were in distress, Nehemiah sought the king's permission to go and help them. From that moment, despite the obstacles and opposition he faced, he was determined to accomplish God's plan to rebuild the city walls to protect the people.

Nehemiah understood that a true vision is God-inspired, God-revealed, and worthy of leadership. This vision, as is often the case, emerged out of a devastating situation. To despair would have been easier, but a great leader always seeks God, especially in difficult times. People are also more willing to follow a leader following God's leading and guidance rather than steps taken by trial and error.

Nehemiah first articulated the vision, but the people bought into it and made their gifts available to achieve what was a monumental task plagued with divisions, hard feelings, and outside opposition. Yet, they persevered faithfully (but not perfectly). Below are some lessons we might learn from Nehemiah's leadership example.

1. He perceived and responded positively to God's call.

God has always called leaders, but few recognize it, and many do not respond positively. Nehemiah recognised a call to action from the information received and immediately seized the opportunity handed to him (Nehemiah 2:12). The burden on his heart translated to the vision God wanted him to act on (1:1-4).

2. He cared more for the people's situation than his own.

Despite being a slave in the king's palace, Nehemiah responded to his people's cries at the expense of his own condition. He also identified with the Israelites by thinking in terms of 'we' and 'us' (2:17, 20) and referred to the situation as 'the trouble we are in' (2:17).

3. He clarified the problem and provided direction

When Nehemiah said, 'You see the trouble we are in, how Jerusalem lies in ruins with its gates burned,' he was assessing the situation the people faced. Without an honest description of the situation, progress is impossible.

'Nothing is more limiting to a group than the inability to talk about the truth[3].' He clarified the problem and then gave direction.

4. He committed to prayer

God speaks into every situation, but if we are not tuned in through prayer, his response and instruction might not reach our hearts.

The information came to Nehemiah suddenly, and the task seemed pressing, but he took the time to pray. The same happened when Jehoshaphat received unexpected information that required an instant response. He immediately created time to place the matter before God (2 Chronicles 20:1-4). The urgency of a matter should never push us into action without ascertaining God's direction and intervention in prayer.

5. He understood and communicated the vision well

People build complicated systems, but God's will is often simple. For Nehemiah and Judah, the vision was represented in three words: 'rebuild the wall'. The people had various needs, hopes, and dreams, but God's vision was captured in rebuilding the wall, without which the other needs could not be met. Nehemiah understood this and was able to carry the people along.

---

3   https://leadershipvoices.com/2013/08/29/courage/

6. He built a team

Nehemiah's gaining the people's trust allowed him to build a team that took shared responsibility for accomplishing the goal. No one, not even Nehemiah, could accomplish this vision alone.

Also, he began with a few people, then expanded the team to include almost everyone in the city. As the people committed themselves to the 'common good' (2:18), individual talents were identified and used, and each person worked on sections of the wall closest to their homes.

> *The urgency of a matter should never push us into action without ascertaining God's direction and intervention in prayer.*

But even God's people get tired. They felt the task was taking too much time and was too difficult. There were internal disputes. It's been said that 'Everything looks like a failure in the middle', but Nehemiah found ways to alleviate the people's concerns without losing sight of the vision, demonstrating a major leadership quality - the ability to raise a healthy and functioning team.

7. He kept the real purpose in sight.

People can get tired and forget the purpose behind the vision while working to fulfil it. Rebuilding the wall was intrinsic to a larger purpose - reclaiming Nehemiah's and Judah's identity as a people of faith. What was at stake was not just a wall (Chapter 8; 12:27), and once Nehemiah reminded the people that their task was tied to a greater purpose, they put their hearts into their work and completed the task in fifty-two days (6:15-16). What an amazing feat!

8. He carried on despite adversity.

Judah's enemies ridiculed, mocked, and did everything possible to discourage them, including lying about Nehemiah's integrity. However, Nehemiah knew he was 'doing great work' (6:3) and refused to be distracted by their debates. God's people cannot give up when adversity comes.

Conclusion

In addition to what Nehemiah's life shows us, a servant-leader must discover the next line of action after completing a task. When people work hard to accomplish a great goal, the temptation is to want to stop and rest. We can celebrate victories, as Nehemiah and his people did, but God is never finished with us. After giving thanks, we regroup and ask God,

'WHAT WOULD YOU HAVE US DO NEXT?'

We are always on a journey with God, and we must stay in pursuit of that new land, goal, or expansion he has in mind. God always has something else on the horizon, and we cannot reach it by remaining where we are.

When the world leaves us confused and questioning, God's word distinguishes fact from fiction. Leadership is no exception. There may not be many godly leadership examples to imitate, but you can go first! Lead like Christ and make your example contagious to those around you. Honour and submit to God's authority; serve, know, and care for others.

This is someone others want to follow.

CHAPTER FIVE

RAISING GODLY LEADERS IN THE CHURCH

Here are some steps for raising godly leaders in the church.

1. SHEPHERD TOWARDS BIBLICAL QUALIFICATIONS

The place to begin is with Paul's list of qualifications in Timothy and Titus:

If anyone aspires to the office of overseer, he desires a noble task. Therefore, an overseer must be:

- » above reproach,
- » the husband of one wife,
- » sober minded,

- » self-controlled,

- » respectable,

- » hospitable,

- » able to teach,

- » not a drunkard,

- » not violent but gentle,

- » not quarrelsome,

- » not a lover of money.

- » Must manage his own household well, with all dignity,

- » keep his children submissive. If someone does not know how to manage his own household, how will he care for God's church?

- » He must not be a recent convert, or he may become puffed up with conceit and fall into the condemnation of the devil.

- » Moreover, he must be well thought of by outsiders so that he may not fall into disgrace, into a snare of the devil. (1 Tim. 3:1–7; Titus 1:6–9)

There's nothing extraordinary about these virtues. But as the picture of maturity for all, the elder should model the Christian life extraordinarily well. The above list (with the exception of the ability to teach) is a good discipling tool and puts the onus on elders to raise up future leaders. That is one of your particular obligations. Paul tells Timothy to look for 'faithful men' who can 'teach others,' as well as men who 'aspire to the office of overseer.' Ultimately, you want to shepherd men toward being biblically qualified. That's the starting point.

2. CAREFULLY OBSERVE FAITHFUL MEN

To raise up leaders, you must continuously watch out for them. Pastors should be profoundly opportunistic about raising up more pastors. The whole church should have a deep confidence that the Lord wants new leaders to be cultivated (2 Timothy 2:2).

3. SPEND PERSONAL TIME

Jesus called the disciples to join him on the mountain so they might 'be with him.' Pastors who build walls around themselves will struggle to model their leadership style effectively and directly. Without becoming an extrovert, a pastor needs to spend time with other potential leaders in his church. Hebrews 13 exhorts the church to follow their elders' example, but how can they do so without knowing their leaders personally? Paul's call to imitate him also required the same - time spent.

4. ADVANCE TRUST

Raising leaders is characterized by a willingness to advance trust. Love believes all things and hopes all things (1 Cor. 13:7). Members of your church will be entrusted with great talent, but someone must advance trust, like credit, to discover their potential. Good leaders do not wait for people to prove themselves before providing teaching opportunities. No, they see the hint of something that, with a little encouragement, could grow and flourish.

> *Pastor Eddie exemplifies the principles of transformational leadership, creating an extraordinary vision and instilling a sense of purpose that resonates with everyone he encounters. You cannot cross paths with him and remain the same.*
>
> *For one thing, he recognised and nurtured my spouts of creativity until they became my passion. As a leader of leaders, he raised me to see my true value and took me from being a 'behind the scenes' shrinking violet to a confident leader of many teams. He taught me how to lead with love, recognise individual strengths and create a collaborative culture that breeds success, which is his forte.*
>
> *Pastor Eddie's way of inspiring, motivating, and unlocking hidden potential transcends 'now' to seeing the end, while his charismatic communication and genuine concern for growth elevated me to new heights and provided a sense of direction in my life.*
>
> **— Bethel Iduoze, daughter**
> *- Head of Media and 35-strong Connect Group leader*

5. DELEGATE RESPONSIBILITY

This point is tied to the previous one. How do you advance trust? By delegating responsibility and opportunity. There are several components to this:

Give people the opportunity to lead.

Keep a list of potential preachers, service leaders, or Sunday school teachers and provide opportunities to lead and teach, empowering them to build God's kingdom. The more strategically you plan this, the smoother the process.

If you were to start your ministry today with ten people, leadership training and development is crucial. There will be moving targets and issues to address, but within those ten people and their families, identify who is willing to learn and start modelling what you do to them.

> *I have always liked to teach (not preach). PE recognised this and gave me the platform to lead the discipleship school in our church. Whenever I discuss resourcing the department with him, he always points me to the right people. This great leadership attribute has helped me lead the department effectively.*
>
> *– Femi Asogbon*

There are three ways of modelling leadership –

- **Watch me do it** - Get on with the task with everyone observing. When we started our ministry, I explained that I was the chief usher, chief worship leader, and chief Sunday School teacher in our church, meaning our growing congregation could learn how to do these things from watching their pastor. This also placed the onus on me to always be the best example. I couldn't excuse myself for not serving with grace and humility because I was having a bad day.

- **Let's do it together** - Here, we start dividing the previously modelled tasks. Prospective Leader A (PLA) does one task, and I do the other. Then, we get together for feedback on how PLA got on. At this point, PLA is also able to use his initiative, and we discuss this during feedback. PLA is developing his own leadership style in this area while taking along what has been modelled for him.

- **Now you take the lead** – With the confidence that PLA is effective in his role, the tasks are handed off to him and at that point, I would be saying, while you are at it, show Prospective Leader B (PLB) what you are doing and how. Then, the leadership development cycle continues.

6. GIVE AND RECEIVE FEED-BACK

Running alongside delegation and opportunities to minister should be structures for feedback. Model this by showing those you're discipling how to give and receive critique (not criticism) in a godly way. Giving godly encouragement, even where it may seem trivial, is a must, but be honest and tender about areas where improvement is required. Invite and receive their feedback on your leadership styles and model and how you are influencing them. This can only enhance your relationship in the long run.

Paul had several problems with the Corinthian church, yet

I overcame cultural differences, contempt from other Christians, and variable spiritual capacity by changing my perspective about people, seeing them as Jesus Christ does, meeting their needs, and through frequent intercession.

I constantly challenge myself to be better than yesterday and am always open to constructive feedback and advice. I learn from those above me and apply the skills and knowledge to those around me.

*— **John Kajoba***

he started out by thanking God for them (1 Corinthians 1:5, 7). Without flattering the Corinthians, he could acknowledge what God had done. What comes from God belongs to God, like the evidence of grace in one another's lives. Encouraging would-be leaders can teach them to give praise to God.

7. ENCOURAGE GODLY AUTHORITY

Too often today, people don't understand what a gift this can be. Raising great leaders requires us to teach about and encourage godly authority, just as Jesus taught his disciples:

> 'But Jesus called them together and said, 'You know that the rulers in this world lord it over their people, and officials flaunt their authority over those under them. But among you, it will be different. Whoever wants to be a leader among you must be your servant, and whoever wants to be first among you must become your slave' (Matt. 20:25–27 NLT).

The fallen world both misuses and lies about the right use of authority. Satan told Adam and Eve that God could not love them and tell them 'No'. People gravitate towards healthy authority that blesses, nourishes and spends itself for those under its care instead of using them. Just as Jesus tutored his disciples in the godly use of authority and modelled it himself, so must we with those we are developing.

8. EXPECT CLARITY

Church leaders must be uncompromisingly clear when it comes to doctrine and teaching the truth, as Paul taught the Ephesian leaders in Acts 20:27-31 and throughout his letters to Timothy and Titus.

Leaders must be clear-headed about the truth and possess a natural ability to answer the question, 'Why?' And they need to be especially clear about certain issues: the most basic matters of theology and the gospel, those doctrines that distinguish your church from others, and those teachings in Scripture that are under fire and unpopular in the world at large.

9. FOSTER A CULTURE OF HUMILITY

Humility (which drives out envy) is the bedrock for the eight practices listed above. It's unhealthy to watch someone else ministering while thinking, *I am better at this*, or simply feeling discouraged. Think of the instruments in an orchestra. Why would the trombone be jealous of the kettledrum, the bass envy the cello, or the first and second violins compete against each other? Each can be enjoyed for what it is, and a good leader helps everyone to locate his place.

In general, humility helps us speak and stay silent appropriately and be tender-hearted and thick-skinned as needed. God's church will prosper in the hands of humble leaders. What a joy to be used by God to disciple others!

Helpful principles for raising godly leaders:

1. PRINCIPLE:

The call to Christian leadership must come from God and be evident

- o Jesus prayed before selecting even the first disciple.

- o His purpose was that they be 'with him' and share in his public ministry with genuine spiritual authority.

- o He chose unlikely candidates with major differences in character, political bias, social status, and age.

- o He established a senior team (Peter, James, John).

Suggestions for Developing Leaders Today

- o No matter how urgent the need is, do not select and train a leader without first hearing from God (1 Timothy 5:22).

Then make a choice by relying on God's guidance, gifting, and timing.

o Be confident about God's call on their lives despite appearances (John 7:24).

o Choose Christians with proven track records based on their authentic relationships with God ahead of their talents (Acts 6:3; Titus 1:6-9).

o Encourage new believers to grow in Christ before thrusting them into ministry (1 Timothy 3:6).

o Even if they are not your mirror image, cherish each person's distinctiveness and work with them individually.

o Work out the levels of individual coaching each one needs.

o Do not allow favouritism to drive your decisions (Luke 20:21, 1 Timothy 5:21).

> *Having recognised my passion for children's ministry, Pastor Eddie asked me to lead our Junior Church. He was always open to my ideas for making Junior Church better and more effective, providing support and resources as needed. Knowing my pastor understood the importance of every aspect of ministry, in this case, the children's ministry, helped me to lead with conviction.*
>
> *To increase my effectiveness as a leader, I continually reflect on my leadership outcomes, review who I am leading, how I am leading, and to what end. I am committed to self-development in all aspects of my life and, to this end, constantly seek out helpful resources.*
> **– Gladys Asogbon**

2. PRINCIPLE:

To be effective, God's servant must be totally surrendered

'Follow me' (Mark 1:7) is,

- o A call to die to self and follow Christ (because He would first die for them).

- o An immediate call (Matthew 8:20, 21) – a deferred response is a negative response.

- o A call to absolute surrender - 'We have left all and followed you.' (Luke 18:28)

Suggestions for Developing Leaders Today:

o Urge everyone to take God's calling seriously.

o Help them see that they are called by God, not people or position (Hebrews 5:4).

o Help them process the 'cost' of commitment to Christian leadership/ service.

o Explain the 'why' of Christian ministry (Matthew 17:1).

o Model how to hear from God regularly and respond with willing obedience.

o Show them that Christian ministry goals are eternal and not defined by human measures of 'success'.

o Help them clarify, develop and validate the nature of their call.

o Involve them in your life.

o Help them understand the benefits of team dynamics/ synergy (and the blessing God promises where there is unity) and how to develop such relationships.

3. PRINCIPLE:

Christian leadership must be based on the truth

- o Information - 'The Kingdom of God is like ....'

- o Explanation. 'I will instruct you.' Jesus 'spoke' to many crowds but 'taught' the disciples:

- how to pray with discipline, based on a dynamic relationship with God

- the true meaning of his public teaching, e.g., in the parables

- the true meaning of the life of faith

- the nature of the church and its redemptive mission

- the spiritual nature of leadership (sacrifice, not control - Matthew 20:25-27)

- to be tolerant of other ministries

- how to manage relationships the right way.

He also balanced private instruction with on-the-job training.

Suggestions for Developing Leaders Today

o   Give them good teaching material from a wide variety of sources.

o   Teach them what you know. Be patient and generous; you are investing in a life.

o   Help them develop solid learning skills.

o   Help them understand how to 'rightly divide the word of truth' (2 Timothy 2:15) and discern between truth and error.

o   Help them develop skills and reinforce 'truth' in those they lead.

o   Take them with you into ministry situations, then explain the work.

o   Give them practical ministry learning opportunities and help them grow from the experiences.

4. PRINCIPLE:

Christian leadership must be based on Christ's example

- o 'Watch me do the work, then copy me': modelled by practical examples from his relationship with the Father (personal relationship, dependency, obedience).

- o Supernatural ministry, godly character, humility (Matthew 11:29; John 13:4-10).

- o He called the disciples to live and travel with Him, and they experienced His lifestyle first-hand for several years.

- o He was a 'friend' but also 'Master' (John 13:13),

- o He exemplified the life of faith and godly values in daily living.

Suggestions for Developing Leaders Today

o   First, ensure your example of Christianity (quite apart from your ministry position or role) is worth following.

o   Share often about how God is shaping you as a Christian leader.

o   Create regular opportunities to share your ideas, programs, style, dreams and challenges.

o   Have ongoing personal conversations with everyone in the leadership group.

o   Where possible, seek to 'father' those you are growing as leaders. Have regular planned and unplanned discussions where you:

-   pray with them and help them deal with setbacks

-   challenge them to go further than required

-   care for them

-   are open with them

-   demonstrate your interest and trust in them

-   help mould their perspectives around Jesus Christ.

5. PRINCIPLE:

God will test leaders for full effectiveness

After three years of close contact with Jesus and witnessing his power and authority, life and message, there was still no guarantee that the disciples could succeed him. Jesus

- o put no confidence in people (John 2:24, 25)

- o knew one of his team would betray him (John 6:64)

- o Forgave those who struggled but repented (Luke 22:31, 32)

- o Used the disciples' individual quirks to teach and develop them.

- o Tested their motives when it came to their attitudes toward possessions (Matthew 8:20) and notions of power.

- He modelled 'service' (Mark 10:44-46; Luke 22:26, 27)

- inverted hierarchical systems, proving that godly leadership is not merely 'Christian' badging of secular models

- demonstrated that leadership is a 'calling', not something to be 'grasped'

- modelled self-preservation (Luke 8:22-25 - the storm was not an accident)

- explained that rewards must come from God (John 12:26).

Suggestions for Developing Leaders Today

o Channel discussions about position, power, privilege, service, sacrifice and giving.

o Do not lower spiritual qualifications or Scriptural standards.

o Explain the part testing and trials play in every leader's development.

o Teach them to identify learning opportunities in every situation.

o Be patient, forgiving, and redemptive in your discipling.

6. PRINCIPLE:

Spiritual authority and release mark genuine Christian leadership

- o Jesus called His disciples to 'become' ministers, e.g. fishers of men, by imparting his vision and authority.

- o He taught them that true spiritual authority comes from God, gave them permission, authority (Mark 6:7), and spiritual power, and sent the apostles, 'the sent ones,' as well as the seventy, to do what He had been doing (Matthew 10:1, Luke 10:1).

- o 'Go into all the world and make disciples', Jesus' final command before he ascended (Mark 16:15), commissioned them to look after His church.

Suggestions for Developing Leaders Today

- o Give them a godly vision.

- o Help them identify the specifics of God's call.

- o Get them involved in active ministry - give them intense on-the-job training, stretch them, and provide opportunities to test their gifts and make mistakes.

o Do all you can to help them succeed and remain on track.

o Include them in planning and decision-making.

o Expose them to great men and women of God.

o Help them manage conflict with humility and confidence.

o Ensure (through discussion) that they understand the nature and scope of the tasks you assign them.

o Help them 'keep their eye on the ball' and operate within their call (there are many distractions).

o Delegate/release and debrief them after ministry opportunities.

7. PRINCIPLE:

Christian leadership lacks purpose and power without the Holy Spirit's anointing

- o Jesus' initial and ongoing anointing was visible to all and modelled reliance on his anointing by the Holy Spirit (Matthew 12:28; Luke 4:14).

- o He taught them to depend on the Holy Spirit as their sole source of ministry power.

Suggestions for Developing Leaders Today

- o Do not rely on your ministry experience, contacts, wisdom, intuition, or force of personality, but on the Holy Spirit.

- o Actively teach those you are training to listen to the Holy Spirit and live in obedience to Him.

- o Encourage them to allow the Holy Spirit to do God's work in and through them.

- o Teach them how to walk in the Spirit and not let secular values and models hijack their thinking.

o   Teach them how to exercise their spiritual gifts through the Holy Spirit's power.

8. PRINCIPLE:

The goal of authentic Christian leadership is to fulfil Christ's global mission

o   Jesus adapted his message to the times without compromise (Acts 1:8).

o   His theology emphasised taking the message to the world without being bogged down by tradition, place, structures or mood (Mark 1:38).

o   He did not shut himself off from society or contemporary events.

Suggestions for Developing Leaders Today

o   Ask the Holy Spirit to give you a heart for mission, and don't be side-tracked or frozen in time, place, methodology or status.

o   Instil a similar vision in your leaders by involving them in missions within and beyond your community.

- o Bearing the Gospel's unchanging message in mind, develop strategies to keep up with current events and teach emerging leaders to do likewise.

- o Get outside your comfort zone frequently and take your team with you.

9. PRINCIPLE:

Authentic Christian leaders invest in Next-Generation leadership

- o Jesus built solid disciples, filled them with the Spirit, and then released them as leaders and teachers so that the work would continue long after them.

- o His teaching was duplicable.

Suggestions for Developing Leaders Today

- o Keep growing as a healthy Christian (you can't give what you do not have).

- o Understand that developing others is part of your call.

- o Build leadership development into the church calendar.

o   Review what the church is supposed to be and identify gaps (avoid labelling people as 'lay' ministers).

o   Multiply your ministry principles and life experiences by training leaders to teach Bible-based doctrines (2 Timothy 2:2).

o   Avoid using teaching examples that are difficult to follow and imitate.

o   Work with them till you are confident in their ability and integrity (see 2 Corinthians 7:13-16).

o   Leave a legacy (unlike Joshua's generation, see Judges 2:10).

CHAPTER SIX

CHRIST'S TEACHINGS ON HUMILITY

The four Gospels reveal that Jesus walked among men without pride, arrogance, or vanity. Likewise, his words reflected his dependence on the Father.

HIS WORDS ON HUMILITY

From the Sermon on the Mount (Matthew 5:3, 5, 9):

> '...blessed are the poor in spirit, for theirs is the kingdom of heaven...
>
> 'And blessed are the meek, for they shall inherit the earth...

> 'And blessed are all the peacemakers, for they
> shall be called the children of God.'

When the disciples asked him who was the greatest in the kingdom of heaven, Jesus responded by calling a little child to him:

> 'Whosoever … shall humble himself as this little child, the same is greatest in the kingdom of heaven' (Matthew 18:1, 4).

> 'For he that is least among you all, the same shall be great' (Luke 9:48).

Jesus always pointed to the Father as his source of power and knowledge. In the temple during the Feast of Tabernacles, he stated, 'My doctrine is not mine, but his that sent me… He that speaketh of himself seeketh his own glory: but he that seeketh his glory that sent him, the same is true, and no unrighteousness is in him' (John 7:16, 18).

And later, 'I do nothing of myself; but as my Father hath taught me, I speak these things … for I do always those things that please him. … And I seek not mine own glory' (John 8:28–29, 50; see also John 12:49–50).

The Master Teacher frequently warned against pride. During dinner at the home of one of the chief Pharisees, Jesus discerned that each person seated at the table considered themselves better than the other (Luke 14:7[4]). He taught them a parable and then said, 'Whosoever exalteth himself shall be abased; and he that humbleth himself shall be exalted' (Luke 14:11; Luke 18:14).

Jesus demonstrated divine humility during his final moments with the disciples as they walked to the Mount of Olives right before His arrest and Crucifixion: 'I am the true vine, and my Father is the husbandman... He that abideth in me, and I in him, the same bringeth forth much fruit: for without me ye can do nothing' (John 15:1, 5).

A short while later, in His great Intercessory Prayer, He stated:

> 'Father, the hour is come; glorify thy Son, that thy Son also may glorify thee... I have glorified thee on the earth... And the glory which thou gavest me I have given them [His disciples]; that they may be one, even as we are one' (John 17:1, 4, 22).

HIS EXAMPLE

From his birth, the Creator of all things demonstrated humility by condescending to be born into humble

---

4   see Joseph Smith Translation

circumstances (John 1:3). He entered mortality in an animal shelter and slept in a crib used for feeding those animals. Even his first visitors were humble shepherds (Luke 2:7–20).

As Jesus performed miracles in Galilee and his fame spread throughout the regions, people flocked to him, some to be healed, while others were curious. He often told the sick and afflicted, 'Your faith has made you whole,' emphasizing the healed person's role in the miracle instead of the Healer's. After performing the miracles, he often prohibited the healed person from disclosing what happened (see Mark 1:44). He displayed a deeply held desire for his works to remain private.

After he fed the 5,000, the onlookers wanted to crown him king, which would have tempted or corrupted most people, but Jesus ignored them and left for a mountain to be alone (John 6:15). On another occasion, as Jesus rode triumphantly into Jerusalem on a donkey - a recognized Messianic symbol of humility (Zechariah 9:9) - the crowds shouted accolades and spread their cloaks and tree branches before him (Matthew 21:8–9).

Finally, during the hours of his greatest suffering, Jesus subjected himself to the Father and was hung on the cross. His last words typified his teachings on humility. After uttering the words, 'It is finished' (John 19:30), he proclaimed the Father's will was completed, bowed his head, and gave up the ghost.

OUR WORDS AND ACTIONS:

Jesus taught us the meaning of humility in words and examples. Our words and deeds should reflect an inner sense of meekness, contriteness, and submission to the divine will.

WHAT IS HUMILITY?

Humility is the perspective that we are created by and accountable to God, which requires the correct view of God as the supreme Creator and authority in relation to his creatures. Being humble means not being preoccupied with self or a person's lowliness but with God and his highness, followed by self with God in the picture. Put another way, pride led to humanity's fall when Adam and Eve desired to 'be like God' (Genesis 3:5). Humility embraces the reality that we are to obey God's commands, which is what we see in Christ.

Humility, then, is a posture of life that acknowledges and embraces God's goodness and the insufficiency of self.

Christ Humbled Himself

In moving heaven to earth, the divine Son emptied himself, not of divinity (as if that were possible), but of divinity's privileges, becoming subject to human boundaries and limitations. Jesus Christ could have overridden creation's rules and realities, but he took on our humanity instead.

His emptying was not by subtraction (of divinity) but by addition (of humanity): 'taking.'

By Becoming Obedient

So, first, Jesus became a man. Then, as Paul confirms,

> 'And being found in human form, he humbled himself by becoming obedient to the point of death, even death on a cross' (Philippians 2: 6-8)

How did Jesus 'humble himself'? By becoming obedient. To do so, he took 'the form of a servant, being born in the likeness of men' (Philippians 2:7). His identification with humanity meant that Jesus was not spared our frustrations, limitations, and pains. He was all in - fully human in body, mind, heart, will, and surroundings – and humanly vulnerable to the worst this sinful world had to offer. Neither was he spared the ultimate essence of humanity: being accountable to God.

'Although he was a son,' Hebrews 5:8-9 explains, 'he learned obedience through what he suffered. And being made perfect, he became the source of eternal salvation to all who obey him.'

We must obey our Creator just as our Brother did.

To the Point of Death

This self-humbling does not stop at obedience but goes on 'to the point of death.' Christ's obedience was all the way. He did not obey for as long as it was comfortable before trying another path. Humility continues to obey, even as the cost increases. It doesn't say,

'I will obey until I've had enough, and then I'll do it my way.'

It says, 'Your way, all the way to the end, God.'

Jesus' acknowledging and obeying his Father's will by dying on the Cross is how Paul illustrates that most remarkable claim that he 'humbled himself.'

Christ shows us that true humility does not denigrate humanity but makes God's image shine in its fullness. It does not make us less than human; rather, pride is the cancer that corrodes true dignity. Humbling ourselves brings us, step by step, to the bliss and full flourishing for which we were made.

Christ's humility also indicates that God's command is something he has experienced. As lonely as we may feel in our most humbling moments, Christ has been there and is there with us, fulfilling his pledge to 'be with you always' (Matthew 28:20), and all the more tangibly at life's hardest times. He draws near in your humbling, releasing you to receive and welcome the Father's righteousness, learn and chart a new course with his guidance and presence.

This humility in Christ's life, death and resurrection also testifies to one of God's clearest and most memorable promises in the Scriptures. God humbles the proud and exalts the humble. Christ humbled himself, and 'God has highly exalted [literally, super-exalted] him' (Philippians 2:9, words in brackets mine). God will, without exception, exalt those who are his in Christ.

God places a premium on the humble heart and answers its prayers.

- Are you willing to lay aside earthly fame to gain the greatest prize - Jesus himself?

- Are you prepared to go unnoticed with no fanfare or recognition and even be misunderstood?

- Will you walk humbly like Jesus to gain much more in eternity?

'For everyone who exalts himself will be humbled, and he who humbles himself will be exalted' - (Luke 14:11).

CHAPTER SEVEN

CHRIST'S TEACHING ON GIVING

People often question the basic biblical principles for Christian giving. To answer that question and assess our own giving, let's review those principles here.

First, let's examine God's Word without comment:

> 'Beware of practising your righteousness before men to be noticed by them; otherwise, you have no reward with your Father who is in heaven. So, when you give to the poor, do not sound a trumpet before you, as the hypocrites do in the synagogues and in the streets, so that they may be honoured by men. 'Truly I say to you, they have their reward in full. But when you give to the poor, do not let your left hand know what your right hand is doing, so that your giving will

be in secret; and your Father who sees what is done in secret will reward you.' Matthew 6:1-4 'Now concerning the collection for the saints, as I directed the churches of Galatia, so do you also. On the first day of every week each one of you is to put aside and save, as he may prosper, so that no collections be made when I come.' 1 Corinthians 16:1-2

'For you know the grace of our Lord Jesus Christ, that though He was rich, yet for your sake He became poor, so that you through His poverty might become rich. I give my opinion in this matter, for this is to your advantage, who were the first to begin a year ago not only to do this, but also to desire to do it. But now finish doing it also, so that just as there was the readiness to desire it, so there may be also the completion of it by your ability.

'For if the readiness is present, it is acceptable according to what a person has, not according to what he does not have. For this is not for the ease of others and for your affliction, but by way of equality - at this present time your abundance being a supply for their need, so that their abundance also may become a supply for your need, that there may be equality; as it is written, 'He who gathered much did not have too much, and he who gathered little had no lack." 2 Corinthians 8:9-15

'Now this I say, he who sows sparingly will also reap sparingly, and he who sows bountifully will also reap bountifully. Each one must do just as he has purposed in his heart, not grudgingly or under compulsion, for God loves a cheerful giver.' 2 Corinthians 9:6-7

PRINCIPLES OF CHRISTIAN GIVING

1. The Lord Jesus requires us to give.

Jesus told his disciples, *'When* you give...' not *'if* you give...' (Matthew 6:2). Giving is essential, not optional, for the Christian. People will often say: '...they had to give in the Old Testament, but in the New, we only give if we want to.' This is clearly not what Jesus taught. He expected his followers to be givers. **Do you give?**

I teach on giving as part of stewardship and spiritual maturity by talking about the Three Ts.

Give of your Time, Talent, and Treasure. We are stewards in these three areas. So, we should give of our time to God by using our talents and also giving of our treasures. As a church we teach the people to tithe 1 out of 10. You are giving 1 out of your 10 to God. If a person cannot give 1 out of 10, the problem is more than the tithe. I remember preaching once from a different angle. During the service, I said,

'It's fine if you don't want to tithe. But as a parent of, say, four children, why not calculate the cost of 'childcare' and teaching during the service, for your four children? How about the comfort you enjoy each week you attend the church – air conditioning, comfortable seating, and of course, the message you hear which sets you up for the week and life? Put a cost to that and pay that instead of your tithe.'

After the service, a gentleman approached me.

'Pastor, I have never believed in tithing,' He said. 'But after doing the maths as you suggested, I will start tithing from now on.'

Think about it this way. No one goes with their family of six to eat at a restaurant and walks out without paying and often, including a tip. Why does it feel right to do so at church where you receive your spiritual nourishment? Even if you only went into McDonalds to use their facilities, you feel obliged to buy a portion of chips.

2. The Lord Jesus wants us to give for the right reasons.

Jesus warned the disciples not to give for men's recognition. 'Beware of practicing your righteousness before men to be noticed by them' (Matthew 6:1). We should always examine our motives and ensure that we are acting for God's glory and seeking his approval of our giving, not people's praise and admiration. **Are you giving for God's or man's approval?**

3. We are to practice charitable giving.

When Jesus said, 'When you give to the poor...' (Matthew 6:2-3), he was teaching about 'alms': aid, charity, or benevolent offerings for the needy. **Do you give amply enough so the Church can be generous in benevolent giving?**

4. Our giving is ultimately to the all-seeing heavenly Father.

'When you give...your Father who sees what is done in secret will reward you' (Matthew 6:3-4). We are not merely adding to the Church budget by giving; it's a thanks offering to the Father. In giving 'as unto the Lord', our goal is to please him. **Are you conscious that you are giving to and seen by the Lord?**

5. Christian giving is an act of worship.

The above truth is expressed differently in Paul's words to the Corinthians, 'On the first day of every week, each one of you should set aside a sum of money in keeping with your income, saving it up....' (1 Corinthians 16:2 NIV). Taking up the collection forms part of their regular Lord's Day worship in accordance with God's word. Paul speaks here of a 'collection for the saints' – the Church giving to the Church for the Church. **Did you realize that giving is a part of worship? Is your worship abundant or inhibited in this area? Do you prioritise giving to the Church?**

6. Christian giving should be done in light of the Incarnation.

Many Christians argue about whether the tithe (10% of our income) is still the standard for our giving to the Church (those against usually lean towards less), but Paul scuttles the whole debate in one verse:

> 'For you know the grace of our Lord Jesus
> Christ, that though He was rich, yet for your
> sake, He became poor, so that you through His
> poverty might become rich' (2 Corinthians 8:9).

Christ's self-giving is now our standard! We are to aim beyond the tithe and emulate his self-sacrifice. Our giving is to be inspired and instructed by Christ's inexpressible gift. With such a challenge, who could possibly satisfy himself by asking, 'How little can I acceptably give?' **Do you try to give as little as possible, or do you bear Christ's costly sacrifice in mind?**

7. Christian giving should be according to our means.

Paul is quite clear on this. 'For if the readiness is present, it is acceptable according to what a person has, not according to what he does not have' (2 Corinthians 8:12). You should give in proportion to what God has given you. He said it this way in 1 Corinthians 16:2, '...each one of you is to put aside and save, as he may prosper.' This means at least two things:

1. We should give proportionately, so those with more money give more [we who are materially blessed must remember this], and

2. The Lord never asks us to give what we do not have or to contribute beyond our means.

Are you giving in proportion to the material blessings you have received?

8. God's blessings are connected to how liberally we give.

Jesus and Paul both emphasize the correlation between giving to God and receiving from him. While Paul says, 'Now this I say, he who sows sparingly will also reap sparingly, and he who sows bountifully will also reap bountifully' (2 Corinthians 9:6 NLT), Jesus reminds us, in Matthew 6:4, that the reward for giving comes from our heavenly Father. As someone once said: 'The desire to be generous and the means to be generous both come from God.' **Are you aware that the Lord gave you much, so you can give much?**

> *'The desire to be generous and the means to be generous both come from God.'*
> **- Author unknown**

9. Giving must be done willingly.

We learn this in 2 Corinthians 9:7, 'Each one must do just as he has purposed in his heart, not grudgingly or under compulsion.' But doesn't this contradict the first principle that Christian giving is not optional? No, true Christian giving is both mandatory and voluntary in that it is required by God but always willingly given by the believer. **Do you give to the Church wholeheartedly, indifferently, or grudgingly?**

10. Christian giving should be done cheerfully.

'God loves a cheerful giver.' With this amazing assertion, Paul assures us that the Lord especially delights in joyful, energetic, merry givers. **Is there joy in your heart when you give? Are you a 'cheerful giver'?**

The Church has not come close to our full potential in giving. Why not pray for us to give with the right motives, joyously and extravagantly?

JESUS TEACHES ABOUT GIVING

'Be careful! When you do good things, don't do them in front of people to be seen by them. If you do that, you will have no reward from your Father in heaven.'

'When you give to the poor, don't be like the hypocrites. They blow trumpets in the synagogues and on the streets so that people will see them and honour them. I tell you the truth, those hypocrites already have their full reward. So, when you give to the poor, don't let anyone know what you are doing. Your giving should be done in secret. Your Father can see what is done in secret, and he will reward you.'
Matthew 6:2-4

GOD IS MORE IMPORTANT THAN MONEY.

'Don't store treasures for yourselves here on earth where moths and rust will destroy them, and thieves can break in and steal them. But store your treasures in heaven where they cannot be destroyed by moths or rust and where thieves cannot break in and steal them. Your heart will be where your treasure is... No one can serve two masters. The person will hate one master and love the other or will follow one master and refuse to follow the other. You cannot serve both God and worldly riches.' Matthew 6:19-21, 24

CHAPTER EIGHT

HOW I LEARNED TO LEAD LIKE JESUS

My leadership journey dates back to my childhood and came about by default. I was the eldest son of eight children. Being a firstborn male was a big deal, and respect was fundamental to how our family operated. My mother consistently reminded me of my responsibilities from the age of nine:

'Lead your siblings by example.'

'Set an example for your brothers and sisters.'

'They are all watching you.'

'If you fail, they have all failed.'

As the firstborn male, if I was sleeping, you had to wake me up gently. You couldn't shout or shake me vigorously. The thought behind this was that you don't become a king after you arrive on earth; you are born a king, and you have to be treated as such. You might think this was much pressure for a kid, and I probably did, too. But leadership starts from self-awareness. Understand your role within the context you find yourself and then live up to it.

The next stage was when I became a born-again Christian on July 4th, 1988. After a while, I began asking the Lord a question that inevitably comes to most of us.

What am I doing here? What have you called me to do?

We all ask this question at one point or another in life. For me, it shaped my journey significantly because God answered clearly from 1 Timothy 4:12:

> '... set an example for the believers in speech,
> in conduct, in love, in faith and in purity.'

He then confirmed the instruction through people, events, and other ways. So, I got the message - I was to be an example to believers. My mother's admonitions when I was growing up created that awareness that my life should model leadership and responsibility. So, when God instructed me to be an example to believers, I knew exactly what he meant.

In one sense, that made my mission clear when it came to the church, but I couldn't call it leadership until I moved to the United Kingdom, where the mission statement of Trinity Chapel, the church we joined in 1997, was *Developing Leaders, Influencing Society.* This was my first encounter with the concept of leadership and the word 'leaders' being used in the church. That piqued my curiosity, and I started looking into this idea. Then, I was introduced to John Maxwell's books, followed by his programmes. So, 1997 was a milestone year in my life; I started my first John Maxwell programme and read all his books, the first of which was *The 21 Laws of Leadership* (still highly recommended today). I eventually became a John Maxwell-certified coach.

My journey progressed. At twenty-eight, I was a consultant, manager, and partner in a management training firm, where I had the privilege of leading a team in the Treasury Department. This is quite different from leading people in the church, and it introduced me to corporate leadership. It also exposed me to leading a team and teaching other leaders within a corporate organisation.

My commissioning was apparent from 1 Timothy 4:10-12, Trinity Chapel's *Developing Leaders, Influencing Society* mission statement, and our lead pastor introducing us all to the John Maxwell programmes into which I immersed myself.

I don't recall a clear transition from secular to ministry leadership for a primary reason - people are at the heart of leadership. Leadership is all about helping people, which I have always loved regardless of my field of work. Additionally, self-awareness brings out the situational leader. Leave ten people in a room for two hours, and a leader will emerge. Great leadership is value-driven since values shouldn't change in the boardroom, church or elsewhere. Adding value to people has always been my core understanding of leadership.

DEFINITIONS

What is a good leader?

A good leader considers the interests of others when achieving their objective, while a great leader is committed to raising good leaders.

A servant leader goes further to serve the interests of other people, as opposed to leaders who are self-oriented. He prioritises and gives to the goals and objectives of those around him, but the average (even great) leader can be a taker, using people to predominantly accomplish personal (or even organisational) objectives.

The Servant Leader is a Resource

I primarily see myself as a resource. One way we have grown as a church is that when meeting you for the first time, I have three main thoughts:

- What is your current position?

- Where are you going?

- And how can I help you get there?

In asking these questions, I want to help you reach your God-ordained destination by working out how to plug myself into your journey, goals and objectives.

Instead of initially seeking to achieve my goals, I always flip this around to find out what the individual is about, where they want to get to, and how I can help.

> *A servant leader always presents himself as a resource for others to use.*

For instance, if I meet a publisher for the first time, I immediately think we can have a publishing ministry to resource writers, authors, editors, and proofreaders. This emphasises the concept of what 'every joint supplies to perfect the body of Christ'. As a joint in the Body, I need to be plugged in to bring value to someone else. If I were to describe myself as a body part, I am a hand. So, I am constantly looking for those who need things carried to fulfil that function. The Kingdom of God is a big ecosystem where every human being (especially the born-again spirit-filled Christian) is designed to plug into each other to achieve perfection. The servant leader is searching for the next person into whom the leader can pour himself as a resource.

People are your Assets

> '...may grow up in all things into Him who is the head—Christ—from whom the whole body, joined and knit together by what every joint supplies, according to the effective working by which every part does its share, causes growth of the body for the edifying of itself in love.' - Ephesians 4:16

> The king of Sodom said to Abram, 'Give me the people and keep the goods for yourself' (Genesis 14:21 NIV).

A primary factor for great leadership is understanding the value of those you are called to work with and serve. People are currency. In other words, they are the most valuable assets for any organisation or church. My favourite Scripture verse in Ephesians 4:16 describes the Church (God's people) as joints in Christ's body that can only function efficiently when each person is supplying what they are wired to. So, you and I are part of an ecosystem that will never be complete unless we are interlocking with others. Nothing gets done, and dreams can never be achieved without people. John Maxwell often says even The Lone Ranger had Silver, his horse and Tonto for company. Choose people over material things because they will always create those things.

When I was starting out in ministry, my spiritual father told me in no uncertain terms,

'Don't raise money. Raise people.'

Consider people as valuable assets, and the money and material things will follow.

> *Don't raise money.*
> *Raise people*

Accountants always ensure that a company's human resources department is listed on the balance sheet because the company's staff are indispensable assets. When you lose material things, you are always able to recreate them if you have and raise people.

That Which Every Joint Supplies

I have used this Scripture to start businesses and ministries and to train and raise leaders. It is based on understanding your role within the Body. I usually help people process this by asking the question: if you were to describe yourself using the human anatomy, which part would you be? Since I am a hand, I watch out for those classified as eyes, ears, legs, and other body parts to put together a fully functional team.

An individual who often says, 'I see...', 'I see what you are saying,' or 'I can see XYZ', is usually an eye. Or Jane might be known for language like 'I met someone who can help with this', 'I know just the person to solve that problem', or she happens to know people across different spheres. She may be described as a networker, but I would call her a leg.

> *Leadership is not static. The situations in which we find ourselves provide the environment for leaders to emerge.*

This is an interesting dynamic on many leadership journeys. Many Christians are aware of the Scriptures describing the various body parts as crucial to the body functioning effectively, but often a full understanding of how this works is lacking:

Don't raise money. Raise people

'The human body has many parts, but the many parts make up one whole body. So, it is with the body of Christ.... Yes, the body has many different parts, not just one part. If the foot says, 'I am not a part of the body because I am not a hand,' that does not make it any less a part of the body. And if the ear says, 'I am not part of the body because I am not an eye,' would that make it any less a part of the body? If the whole body were an eye, how would you hear? Or if your whole body were an ear, how

> would you smell anything? ...The eye can never
> say to the hand, 'I don't need you.' The head
> can't say to the feet, 'I don't need you."
> - 1 Corinthians 12:12, 14-17

When that lightbulb goes on, the individuals will inevitably try to categorise themselves, opening up an entirely different conversation. My role as the hand/coach is to sit them down and ask pertinent questions to easily deduce who they are within the Body.

Two kinds of Awareness

No one motivates fish to swim or birds to fly. Knowing who you are, which is self-awareness, is the basis of good leadership, and situational awareness makes for an excellent leader. Ephesians 4:12 teaches us not to overrate ourselves and to remain grounded. One person cannot be the eyes, hands, feet, and every other organ. Each one of us is only one part. The best results come from supplying your own part and working with others who are doing the same.

Self-awareness gives you your identity, and situational awareness makes you an excellent leader. The pandemic destroyed countless organisations, but others grew within the same event because their leaders adapted their skills to the incoming problems. They thrived and hit the ground running on exiting that drawn-out global incident. On the other end of the scale, some organisations simply went under. Many churches closed down, and those who hung in there but failed to adapt really struggled and have not recovered to date.

Excellent leaders can read the room and understand what to do as situations arise. Leadership is not static, and the situations we find ourselves in provide the environment for a leader to emerge.

Israel's war with the Philistines birthed a David. As long as problems occur in the world, leaders will always emerge, but excellent leaders read each situation and adapt accordingly.

We run three services on Sundays. Despite covering the same topic, the approach to each differs because the people in attendance are different. Before picking up the microphone, I scan the room, size up the demographic and ask myself - which language or words will best deliver the message to those in front of me? From their body language, I can immediately tell how best to serve these people. Excellent leaders have a very high level of situational awareness.

The recent pandemic and wars are good examples of situations that bring about excellent leadership. Some people might believe they would do better if the 2020 virus had said, 'Hey, I'm coming in two years' time, or if there was a notification that September 11, 2001, would change history. The same could be said of the Russia/

Ukraine or Israel/Palestine wars. We went to sleep one night, and the global landscape was unrecognisable the following day. The pertinent question on a leader's lips should be, 'What qualities do I need to hear the news and think, 'Ahh, this is how I'm going to step into my day'?

So, what is my definition of leadership? In basic terms, a leader gets people from A to Z.

Human beings are almost always in transit, and life is about movements that are often interjected or interrupted by situations. The question from my approach is always, 'This person needs to move from point A to point B. How do I navigate this interruption and still serve and help her on her journey?'

This leads to another important point – clarifying your goal or objective. Once this is clear, then creativity kicks in. Your experience, education, exposure, the ability to leverage your assets (people), prayers, word of knowledge, and all your skills now become resources to navigate the interjection, enabling the person or organisation to keep progressing on their path. Of course, you may encounter ten people with varying circumstances that will demand from you, the leader, situational awareness and the requisite skills to provide distinct solutions for each.

Wherever you are on your leadership journey, both levels of awareness are pivotal to your destination. Understand each situation and then adapt and adjust.

Be More, Do More, Give More and Build Better is a living concept, designed with continuous self-improvement at heart. It propels a person to discover or rediscover themselves in God's revealed, written, and spoken word.

I regularly self-evaluate using God's word as the yardstick to benchmark whether I have fully applied myself to my tasks and responsibilities. Could I have done more or better? Have I given the task my all? Assessing and ensuring my achievements for the day is building a better tomorrow for me and those around me. Two examples:

A. Family: I have become a better husband and father by leading my family with these principles. The outcome is an incredibly happy wife, a beautiful and peaceful home, and children with outstanding results from a top school in the country.

B. Work: I picked up a small complex service with a team of four and grew the team to thirty-five, and the annual revenue from hundreds of thousands to tens of millions. We are still growing year on year.

It becomes even more rewarding when proteges at work naturally gravitate towards me for coaching and mentoring or when I am tasked to rescue a failing project.

— *Tunde Adeboga*

BE MORE, DO MORE, GIVE MORE, BUILD BETTER – THE FOUR PILLARS OF EXCELLENT LEADERSHIP

Whatever your achievements, there is always more. This is an intrinsic principle in leadership. If you can achieve a goal or objective in one category, you can do two, three and four, and more than that, in different areas. There is always more to be and do. In your marriage, with your children, your life goals, relationships, and finances. There is always much to do. Then, it is also a matter of priorities.

With respect to my being the hand for those who come in contact with me, my job is to also discover their priority and how I can be a massive resource. I then hand myself to them on a platter so they can achieve those things. Other than that, what makes you excellent is the situation and process. No matter how good your plan is, interruptions can occur at any time, so you must understand situations and know what is required.

SIX CORE LEADERSHIP STRENGTHS

Humility

> 'Isn't this the carpenter's son? Isn't his mother's name Mary, and aren't his brothers James, Joseph, Simon and Judas? Aren't all his sisters with us? Where then did this man get all these things?' Matthew 13:55-57

Jesus was notoriously humble. We are told in Philippians that he lowered himself all the way from heaven to become a man. In addition, people initially underrated him and didn't expect much because he freely went about among them, not flaunting himself, discarding all his privileges and spending time with people from all walks of society. This accessibility, humility and being underestimated made Jesus a people magnet.

Many years ago, I decided to become more accessible to everyone in our ministry, so my contact details are widely available. Now, you would think my phone would constantly ring since everyone has the number, but it doesn't. That action expresses confidence that our folks will not take advantage of my trust in them. They recognise my sincerity when I say, 'Call me at any time of the day' and reach out to me with urgent needs. But it never leads to a deluge of calls.

Consistency

This trait and ability mean I am the same person today, tomorrow and the day after. Not nice, reliable, and outstanding today, and mean, undependable and mediocre tomorrow. Consistency creates stability. Some years ago, Roberts Liardon, author of *God's Generals*, visited our church, and afterwards, we went for dinner at a restaurant. The following year, he visited us again, and my wife and I took him to the same restaurant. Halfway through the meal, he looked at me.

'Wow, Pastor Eddie,' he said, 'You are a very consistent person.'

I was taken aback. 'OK…, thank you,' I replied, deciding to take it as a compliment.

'It's one thing I like about you.' He continued. 'You brought me to this same restaurant last year, and you ordered the same meal!'

Hebrews 13:8 tells us Jesus Christ is the same yesterday, today, and forever, which is why we love and trust him. People want a leader who, come rain or shine, will be there for them. There are no concerns about his actions or reactions, and they don't wonder if he will keep his promises. Consistency breeds dependability, and the perception of stability means people have one less concern about the person leading them.

For a dependable pastor, the church member subconsciously thinks, 'I am not concerned about my pastoral needs because I know where my pastor stands. She will support me and my family. She is available, listens to our issues without judging, and is on our side, year in, year out.'

Certain leaders can be described as good or even great, but you cannot count on them. Will they be there next year, in two or three years? No one can be certain.

Today, our ministry consists of different generations. People who joined us over 20 years ago are still members. My daughter serves within the ministry, as do several of those born into our church, and this is all down to consistency and stability. The young people go off to

> PE's consistency has made the most difference to my own leadership journey in three key areas.
>
> 1. Consistency in planning
> 2. Consistency in embracing change
> 3. Consistency in executing
>
> **— Ibukun Onitiju**

university, return and remain with us, in one sense, because Dad or Mum has worked with the pastor and always spoken well of him. On my part, whether I am with a seventeen-, eighteen-, or twenty-year-old, I engage with them at a level unexpected for a fifty-seven-year-old.

Someone of my age wouldn't be expected to pastor them directly, but they are comfortable enough to hang around and chat with me because of that consistency.

This is not always the case in many churches. What you might find is that children attend church with their parents to start with, but once they get to university or can make their own choices, they check out of that church for lack of identification.

Again, this reflects on the range of leadership. There are many great leaders around the church, but the excellent leader addresses such situations before they become problematic for the church.

I understand that there is the potential for generational gaps, so I often tell our church members: 'I am a pastor to you and your children.'

I am just as excited when I see the parents, the ten- or twenty-five-year-olds. That 'uniformity' of treatment tells young and old that they have a place in our midst, and you can almost hear the following thoughts:

'You know what? I belong here.'
'The leader sees and hears me.'

'I'm not just my dad's son in this church. I have that same rapport with the pastor that my dad has.'

That connection leads to a sense of ownership and belonging, without which they start drifting to where they will be seen. Every human being seeks connection, to be seen and heard. The excellent leader reads the situation and provides those connections. Otherwise, you end up with a limited demographic within your ministry.

Consistency says what you are doing now, you will always do. When our congregation was eighty members strong, a recurring question cropped up during church and leadership meetings.

'Pastor, we really love the way our church is right now. You are so accessible, and we feel close to you. Will we be able to remain this way when our membership reaches 100?'

My reply was always the same. 'Yes, we will. Family is the fulcrum of our church, and we will remain a family even when we are more than double that number.'

Then we got past the hundred mark, and the comment came back.

'Oh, Pastor. It's all good now, but when we grow to 200, we won't be able to see or talk to you like this.'
'No, we won't change the way we do things,' I said.

Then we hit 200, and the concern didn't go away. But things didn't change when we hit 300, then 400.

The members were afraid that numerical growth would affect our stability. But it didn't because, despite the changes required, our practices, habits, and values remained consistent.

Consistency says, whatever you do now, you will do in ten years.

Execution

Execution is all about getting things done. Ideas are cheap; execution is king.

A great leader should be a master at implementing ideas. What counts is not the number of ideas we have but the number accomplished, which requires a two-pronged approach.

I am constantly executing one idea or another for our ministry, but that's one cap I wear. The other one is executing an idea with or for the people I serve.

Ideas are cheap; execution is king.

Someone approaches me and says, 'Pastor, I want to do XYZ.' As their hand, I can immediately respond with, 'This is what you need to do. And this is what we're going to do. Your project becomes mine in the sense that I will hold you accountable until you accomplish your objective.'

Great leaders get things done instead of merely thinking or talking about them. Execution is a core strength that gets the job done.

Character

A straightforward definition of character is being the same in public as you are in private. You are who you say you are. Character not only makes you dependable, but you aren't two-faced.

Integrity

'Summing it all up, friends, I'd say you'll do best by filling your minds and meditating on things true, noble, reputable, **authentic**, compelling, gracious....'
Philippians 4:8

Merriam-Webster's dictionary defines integrity as a firm adherence to a code of especially moral or artistic values[5]. In other words, it means being honest, trustworthy, consistent, and true to what is fair and just. Which leads to trust on the part of those you lead. It is also being incorruptible. You are authentic in staying true to yourself and your values – the real deal.

I often share the following story with couples and families. Between 2000-2001, I was working in Germany. Around,

---

5   https://www.merriam-webster.com/dictionary/integrity

2:00 AM in the morning, there was a knock on my door. It was a colleague who was based abroad.

'Hello, Eddie. Can I come in?'

I scratched my head, wondering whether she was drunk or sleepwalking. But her eyes were clear enough. 'Evie (not her name),' I started to say, only for her to barge past me.

'I have a document you need to work on for tomorrow.' She announced, marching towards my bed. Seconds later, she was stripping off her clothes and lying on her back. 'Sleep with me.'

I was too stunned to react at first. Then I turned around, darted after her and stood there blankly, unable to believe my eyes and ears.

She made the offer along the lines of it being a one-night stand, and that we would not see each other again. It was full blown temptation staring me in the face. An attractive woman, out of nowhere, offering to sleep with me when I was bleary-eyed.

In hindsight, I could have started praying in tongues or cried out, *Lord, help me!* Or grabbed and thrown her out of my room.

But I did none of those things. *What is this? What do I do?* Was all I could think. My brain wasn't bringing up any solutions. I stood there dry-mouthed, heart palpitating.

Suddenly, a picture came to mind. It was my wife, broken-hearted, crying helplessly on discovering the betrayal. How would I begin to console her? Where would I start? That image was the only thing to convince me that the momentary event was not worth it.

'I can't do this,' I started saying. 'I can't do this! I just cannot.' I repeated, to her and myself.

Then my brain kicked into gear. *I leave tomorrow! I will be seeing my wife tomorrow!*

Finally, I managed to get her out of the room.

I suffered from PTSD for years after the incident, waking up in the middle of the night in a cold sweat, thinking, *Oh, my God. I fell. I really did this.*

At other times, I would wake up angry from a primal instinct asking me why I didn't do it, followed by tears, as I wondered how I managed to portray myself as a guy who would welcome her into my room. It took almost three years for me to fully recover from the mixed emotions.

Accessibility

As we've said earlier, accessibility is a strong point for an excellent leader. This was something Jesus excelled in – he was accessible to the crowds, to friends, family and his disciples. He had different ways of being so, but ultimately, he freely gave of himself by visiting, eating with, walking towards, and, in the most intimate sense, allowing his friends to lean on him.

SIX PITFALLS TO AVOID

Pride

This is the opposite of humility. God opposes the proud and gives grace to the humble. Ego, self-absorption, and self-conceit are pitfalls a good leader needs to guard against.

Pastor Eddie has the God-given ability to identify and push positively and lovingly for the manifestation of hidden gifts (especially when the gift bearer fails to see it). In my case, he asked me to educate the church community on timely finance-related topics pre-, during, and post pandemic, to lead a bible connect group, and mentor young professionals. I ordinarily would not volunteer for these tasks and unenthusiastically agreed, but they have surprisingly unveiled hidden strengths and abilities that would have remained untapped.

I have learnt to appreciate the challenges and sacrifices that come with leadership, and now appreciate my leaders more. Leadership is not a display of power or flaunting who is in charge to others. It is to serve unreservedly without expecting a thank you. My greatest struggle was saying 'NO' as applicable, but through my pastors' mentorship, I have learned to say 'NO' in love and in a way that enables both parties to walk away happy.
—Jums Oladiran

Lack of decisiveness.

A great leader is decisive. You should be able to put your foot down and, at the same time, exercise fairness.

Lack of interpersonal skills.

Being unable to display trust, respect, and honesty within your teams or to those you lead can be problematic for a leader. It is almost impossible to grow a team without the appropriate interpersonal skills. It is also essential to watch out for your tone – avoid critical statements, sarcasm, and unnecessary and inappropriate banter.

Lack of self-awareness

Some leaders do not understand their value and the impact their words can have. They make utterances that destroy those they serve, unaware that words are inherently powerful and positively or negatively affect the hearer. Knowing how people perceive me and how vulnerable they can be, I am extremely careful in this area.

Lack of empathy

Being out of touch with people's feelings.

Lack of vulnerability.

Certain leaders depict themselves as heroes, but people want to be led by human beings. Jesus showed us his vulnerable side when he left heaven and came to earth as a man. In Gethsemane, we saw his weakness as he cried and said, 'Father, if you are willing, take this cup from me; yet not my will, but yours be done' (Luke 22:42). He was reluctant to go through the pain ahead, demonstrating his vulnerability. People are not truly drawn to leaders who always seem to be invincible.

Our leaders know I am as human as they are. Leading is serving and, for me, portrays who I am: a person held together by God's grace.

Trust and Mistrust

People have to be able to trust you, and vice versa.

The positive traits we have mentioned require trust to make the relationship work. With the proviso that everyone (including the leader) is flawed, there has to be mutual reliance. If people don't believe what they share with you stays with you (confidence), that you will be there for them (support), and you will do what you've promised (commitment), they aren't likely to follow you very far.

In the same vein, you extend confidence by allowing them to fail while working towards their potential, know they are in a safe space as they extend their wings, and learn from you how to develop the traits that take them to their destination, wherever that is. This enables you to get the best out of them. With tasks, for example, you are moving that person onto the stage where you can hand it over to them completely. A leader should be able to work himself out of a job. Also, an excellent leader looks to build at least three levels deep. In other words, have substitutes at varying stages of development.

> *A great leader does two things well: replicates herself on various levels and, ultimately, works herself out of a job.*

Using a football game analogy, only eleven players are required for a match, but twenty-two are taken to the pitch, giving each player a substitute. An excellent leader has someone deputising for him, and that person should be developing someone, making the leadership structure two to three levels deep. A leader operating this way will soon work themselves out of that job, which frees them to step up higher in the call.

Like onion layers, our church is structured such that some of our leaders are in their 50s (my age bracket), others in their 40s, 30s, and possibly twenties.

WHAT WE LEARNED ON OUR LEADERSHIP
JOURNEY WITH PASTOR EDDIE

Pastor Eddie offers a refined system that helped me understand the process of finding your call through the combination of Scripture, the individual heart, and the foundational elements of the God-called leadership role. As I move through different phases of life, I confidently realign myself to God's will for me in that regard.

The second thing that has helped me the most is recognising that true leadership is less about the desire to lead and more about understanding the responsibilities expected of you. What have I struggled with most? I usually don't like taking my eye off the ball with my personal achievements and goals and tend to be conscious of failing to meet my in-built standards when supporting others. However, the **Be More, Do More, Give More and Build Better** philosophy innately balances this in that I never end up stepping back from additional responsibility.

-- Asher Iduoze – Youth leader

I was unaware of my divinely assigned calling or skills until Pastor Eddie identified them.

'Angela, your quietness is a real strength,' He said to me during one conversation. 'I also believe you will one day be a pastor and preacher.'

'That's not for me, Pastor,' I replied immediately. Pulpit ministry was something I never imagined in my future.

Pastor Eddie simply smiled, but without pressure, he started offering me opportunities.

At the same time, we had training, mentoring programs and 1-2-1 discussions in which he encouraged me to use my gifting. There was guidance and correction. My struggle was aligning my view of myself with the leadership qualities Pastor Eddie saw and continues to see in me, however, he recently asked my husband and me to pastor and grow one of our campuses. This was not something that we envisioned doing, but he felt we had it in us, and we are now enjoying the role.

Pastor says Christians should never be average or mediocre, urging us to Be More, *Do More, Give More and Build Better.* I transferred this principle to raising my children because they seemed applicable at school, work, or in their spiritual lives. I believe this is a primary reason they are excelling in these areas.

-- Angela Ogbe

Over the years, Pastor Eddie and I have discussed how leadership applies to me; for instance, how delivering messages from the pulpit differs from work presentations. The former is a spiritual assignment that impacts lives through methodologies like prayer. I have been taught to start, end, and interject messages with prayer, which has defined me as a leader.

One dilemma I faced was handling the transition to spiritually leading my friends. Pastor Eddie taught me to set boundaries and manage this practically by ending every conversation with an offer to pray with the person, for example, which established the requisite spiritual authority.

I have learned from Pastor Eddie that, more than being the most achieving colleague at work, I should be known for my work ethics, as I strive for the extraordinary, resulting in my winning several awards at work.

Dedicating time to my family and being a positive role model has also made me a better husband and father.

-- Ayodele Olusanya

I joined Gateway Chapel intending to be a weekly church member, but Pastor Eddie recognised something in me and set me on the leadership track, giving voice to my ideas, and the go ahead to make them happen with his full support and encouragement. I was soon leading a successful team within the church.

There was also a training and mentoring process to align us with Pastor Eddie and the church's vision. Consequently, I was empowered to become a leader within my workplace and have achieved much more in my career. One of the most powerful principles I have learned is that, to get more from people, empower them to be their best and support their ideas by implementing them. Pastor Eddie listens and implements.

Thankfully, each 'promotion' along the way came with preparatory mentoring sessions. Believing I could do all that was placed in my charge was challenging, but PE and other leaders' support and help emboldened me to do what was needed.

I apply the *Be More, Do More, Give More and Build Better* principles in at least three ways:

Leading by example: which means I always do more than I expect from the team.

Sharing my knowledge: I frequently mentor others, which continues the empowerment circle.

Giving: PE taught me that generosity opens the doors to more, and this works in both my team at work and in church.

-- Bola Eniola

Pastor Eddie is a visionary! He has always been able to cascade God's direction and vision with clarity, focusing on the scale of our mission on Earth. We attended week-long seminars at the University of Oxford (to shape our focus about the society and policies that govern us), frequent breakfast meetings, and even a trip to Singapore, which truly defined 'see and believe'.

The love expressed as I went from member to volunteer felt like a rod. I still remember being told off for missing a mid-week service. I was taken aback – after all, I was only a church member who had recently returned from university. But I was subsequently invited to join the protocol team, which fast tracked my integration. Taking on responsibility changed everything.

Next, I was asked to lead a bible connect group. I had never even attended one meeting, but I accepted the role by faith, thinking, *It will not kill me.* I found the church cultures (especially with my peers) a different level of spirituality to what I considered normal, while the adults were on a whole other spiritual wave.

'Why not create the environment you desire?' My brother advised. 'Remember, you were once like this.'

I decided to connect with more spiritually minded people in my age group. PE's preaching (and practising what he preached) kept me grounded. His messages at the time were about loving and letting people grow in Christ. Church is like a hospital that the broken attend to receive Christ's healing. PE shared several practical steps to achieve this mission. *I* had to grow, and many areas of my life needed improving (and still do).

Be More – being an example to those I lead with timely communication, whether good or bad, improved comms within the protocol team, avoiding guesswork and making us more effective.

Give More – PE taught us to honour those who serve consistently in the Kingdom. Our amazing leaders make this easy, so I encourage my peers to do so. It surprises them when I ask whether they have honoured pastors and ministers other than Pastors Eddie and Bola.

Build Better – After running church connects on zoom with breakout rooms, I introduced social calls at work to integrate new colleagues and increase overall engagement since we all work from home. This has energised and allowed people to connect.

I have many areas to improve on, some of which is from lack of focus. I trust with the current vision and steer from PE, I will be revived to honour God and His people by the power of the Holy Spirit.

-- Bukky Kumolu-Johnson – Bible Connect & Care Leader

When I joined the church in 2003, Pastor Eddie's attitude to church development was striking. He pointed out that the church was not the building but the *people* in it, and he embarked on helping each member identify their purpose within the body of Christ. He empowered members who grasped this perspective with the responsibility and authority to serve as such, equipping and helping them see themselves as ambassadors for Christ in the marketplace.

I joined Gateway Chapel a broken man after some disappointment at my previous church. I initially went through a healing phase followed by the process of understanding that Christianity is a lifestyle, not a religion. The vision for the church also taught me to rebuild my world through God's Word. Pastor Eddie must have been observing me for a while. One day he entrusted me with leadership responsibilities that I was not ready for, insisting that I go ahead, which helped shape my personality and composure. Leading Gateway Academy and heading the Church Board exposed me to several challenges that we discussed and worked through.

Pastor Eddie pushes ministry to the fringes for members to explore their own leadership abilities, freeing him to expand or give attention to other areas of the ministry. One admirable gift of his is the use of 'I see in you' conversations. It's a conversation that might go something like this...

'Hey, Fred. You are very analytical in your thinking. I honestly think it's a gift God has wired into your personality. You may not have thought about this before, but we really need that gift here in Gateway Chapel.'

He then entrusts you with responsibilities to enhance that gift. I have seen this process transform members of our church into great marketplace and church leaders. His mentoring skills kick in with evolving challenges, and each leader is placed on a calendar since leadership development takes time and intentionality. Pastor Eddie gets on the same page at first, then gets out of the way to allow for growth as his leaders make decisions and take action until they become independent. That is how I developed and took my leadership skills from the church to the marketplace.

Be More means becoming the person you are envisioning; Do More is about working harder and aiming for excellence with each task. Give More is drawing from your achievements, and Building Better is learning from the whole experience and making improvements for better results. I effectively applied these principles in leading the Transport team in Lagos State, Nigeria, to make better informed transport plans, decisions, and implementation strategies. My professionalism, diligence, transparency, selflessness, dedication, and working tirelessly implemented processes for planning and implementing transport projects which have attracted international funding, leading to national recognition and my appointment as the commissioner for Transportation in Lagos State from 2019 to 2023.

-- Dr Fred Oladeinde

Pastor Eddie expresses love that connects deeply with individuals, which, if accepted, lets him identify their strengths. He has also developed a framework to help anyone develop and gain valuable experience within the body.

- o   Is there a gap or need to be filled?

- o   Is there something you love doing? (Start doing it for the Body.)

- o   Are you an expert in an area? (Contribute to others in the Body.)

My experiences of serving have further created opportunities to monetize these same skills in the marketplace.

Having a clear vision and roadmap to follow has been most helpful, especially when I have struggled with questions like, 'Am I good enough? Or 'Can I do this?' which Pastor Eddie's guidance and trust help me overcome.

Be More, Do More, Give More and Build Better has been pivotal in my leading teams and my personal life, the longest running theme of which has been my shift from Engineering to Digital and Growth Marketing. My unique circumstances limited my chances initially, but a comment from Pastor Eddie changed my perspective.

'You don't want to climb the ladder to the top and find it leaning against the wrong wall'.

He identified digital marketing skills as a potential growth area and recommended that I explore it, despite my studying Civil Engineering at University, giving me the courage to start again. In the past 15 years, I've been able to Be More, Do More, Give More and Build Better, leading growth marketing teams in various industries and countries.

— **Ibukun Onitiju**

I came to understand my calling during a conversation with Pastor Eddie in 2008. At the time, I was a pioneering pastor of a church, but after a night of discussions, it became clear that my calling was as a marketplace apostle and pulpit teacher of the word.

I struggled at first with my career and family life, but close contact and being mentored by Pastor Eddie brought clarity in both areas, resulting in a better understanding of my business and improved relationships with my wife and son. Some practical steps included:

- Listening to Pastor Eddie's teaching.

- Reading his recommended books - John Maxwell is one main author.

- Private mentoring sessions with life examples to back up the teaching.

- Observing how he handles issues to reinforce the learning.

Pastor Eddie's relationship with Pastor Bola (his wife), Asher and Bethel (their children) is also one way to learn about leading within the family as he provides leadership by example.

Our mentoring sessions and training emphasise success as a journey, not a destination. Pastor Eddie keeps pushing the frontier, which makes me comfortable as a team leader to demand more from myself and my team members, even in a place like Lagos, Nigeria, where most of these growth principles are innovative within the body of Christ.

Ultimately, we work on the total man, not just one area of life. For example, our yearly goals cover family, finances, career, business, and ministry.

— Samuel Omole

What made the most difference to my leadership journey were:

— Opportunities to observe PE at close quarters in 1-2-1 conversations or group settings. The way he spoke about different topics, people, and situations validated and/or challenged my thought patterns and processes, shaping my leadership ideals, approach and thinking.

— Secondly, Pastor Eddie has occasionally pulled me up on wrong actions or bad decisions. While these experiences were not always pleasant or comfortable, on reflection, they reinforced the qualities and expectations of those in leadership. One can become passive about these with time, but those occasions reminded me that Christian leadership requires good morals and character traits.

— Pastor Eddie and the other leaders' open-door policy reassured me that I could tap into the available wealth of knowledge, wisdom, and know-how to succeed in my role.

— Adjusting myself - behaviour, serving style, interactions – and the awareness of being in a new capacity created some tension. How could I be different, or should I even be different? I drew my confidence from what I knew and my nature, telling myself to serve in my new role as I had to date. I also prayed, asking God for wisdom and guidance. In hindsight, I could have discussed my feelings with PE and other mentors.

I have taken on the *Be More, Do More, Give More and Build Better* mantra in a number of ways, starting with my connect group. I needed to know the members' challenges, fears, and other aspects of their lives. Since most people prefer discussing private issues with the senior pastor or senior church leadership, it took more than a year to move us from the group model to becoming a family. In addition, despite my busy and tasking life, I took the following steps:

o   Opened up to my team about my personal challenges and juggling life on all fronts.

o   Offered practical help, spent time with them and, through our discussions, created a gateway to relationships beyond the mundane levels often found in church settings.

o   Advocated that the team encourage one another to grow in attainment, character, prayer lives and other areas while challenging me, too. They could regularly ask how I was implementing what was discussed in church and connect groups. The aim was to boldly inspire and build each other up.

Being quite self-critical, I frequently measure myself against the Scriptures and my mentors to fulfil my potential. I am blessed to have this mentality and people pushing me to better myself through continuous professional development, praying more and other forms of self-improvement. I am still on a journey of discovery. Being selected by a trusted mentor has given me a sense of purpose and direction, and the peace I felt reassured me that I am operating within my gift and calling.

—Tade Efevbera

Actors, A. (2019, April 15). Quotes to inspire the Servant Leader in You
Retrieved November 22, 2023, from https://medium.com/agileactors/ quotes-to-inspire-the-servant-leader-in-you-ac3bb281423a#id_token=eyJhbGciOiJSUzI1NiIsImtpZCI6IjViMzcwNjk2MGUzZTYwMDI0YTI2NTVlNzhjZmE2M2Y4N2M5N2QzMDkiLCJ0eXAiOiJKV1QifQ.eyJpc3MiOiJodHRwczovL2FjY291bnRzLmdvb2dsZS5jb20iLCJhenA: https://medium.com/agileactors/quotes-to-inspire-the-servant-leader-in-you-ac3bb281423a#id_token=eyJhbGciOiJSUzI1NiIsImtpZCI6IjViMzcwNjk2MGUzZTYwMDI0YTI2NTVlNzhjZmE2M2Y4N2M5N2QzMDkiLCJ0eXAiOiJKV1QifQ.eyJpc3MiOiJodHRwczovL2FjY291bnRzLmdvb2dsZS5jb20iLCJhenA

Butler, W. (2013, August 29). Courage.
Retrieved January 2024, from Leadership Voices: https://leadershipvoices.com/2013/08/29/courage/

Maxwell, J. C. (1998). The 21 Irrefutable Laws of Leadership.
Retrieved 11 14, 2023, from https://amazon. com/21-irrefutable-laws-leadership-follow/ dp/0785289356

RECOMMENDED READING

- **15 Invaluable Laws of Growth –**
John C. Maxwell

- **The Power of Servant Leadership –**
Robert K. Greenleaf

- **The 21 Irrefutable Laws of Leadership –**
John C. Maxwell

- **The Servant: A simple story about the true essence of leadership –**
James C. Hunter

- **How Successful People Think -**
John C. Maxwell

- **The Self-Aware Leader -**
John C. Maxwell

- **Leader Shift -**
John C. Maxwell

Much of what is said and written about Christian leadership today focuses on theology, hermeneutics, communication, and other skills, with a growing trend of 'celebrity' or secular models. However, Jesus Christ, the most powerful servant-hearted leader to have lived, should be our example.

In *Lead Like This!* Eddie Iduoze encourages Church and marketplace leaders to observe and emulate Jesus' leadership styles and qualities as the standard.

Lead Like This! provides answers to questions like:

- How do I recognize good or great leadership?

- Did Jesus have a preferred leadership style?

- How do I become a great leader?

- What are the pitfalls to avoid?

However long you have been in leadership, the framework and examples in this book will help you recognise what it means to be called, anointed, and raised by God to lead His people.

ABOUT THE AUTHOR

172

Eddie Iduoze is an author, entrepreneur, and business coach. He is also the founding pastor at Gateway Chapel.

A John Maxwell Certified Team Coach, he is passionate about developing and stewarding people through life, and his writing, seminars, coaching, and mentoring programmes are designed to shift them into their purpose.

Eddie is a husband and dad of two and a father figure to many.

www.ingramcontent.com/pod-product-compliance
Lightning Source LLC
Chambersburg PA
CBHW060925140726
47996CB00001B/384